Editorial Direction
JOHN & SARAH WISEMAN

Project Coordinator
BRIDGET GALSWORTHY ESTAVILLO

Graphic Design
EDUARDO ZAPATA GOSSELÍN
JESÚS LAVEAGA TOSTADO
JUDITH MAZARI HIRIART
PRINTT DISEÑADORES, S.C.

Editor
VÍCTOR MANUEL MENDIOLA

Editorial Coordination
MICHAEL CALDERWOOD

Picture Research
JEANNETTE PORRAS PADILLA

Circulation Consultant
BRIAN WEINER

Tequilier
RICARDO CISNEROS BELTRÁN

Illustrations
CARMEN PARRA

Map
ANA MARÍA GARCÍA

Recipes
MARÍA DOLORES TORRES YZÁBAL

Food Stylist
LAURA B. DE CARAZA

Prop Stylist
MARIANA HAGERMAN

Photographic Assistant
MARCO VINICIO CALDERÓN

Translation
JENNIFER CLEMENT

Jacket front: The classic margarita cocktail (see also page 169).
Jacket back: A lone cactus surrounded by agave plants (see also pages 28-29).
Pages 2-3: The Tequilán volcano, Jalisco.
Left: Landscape on the outskirts of the city of Tequila.

*First published in the United States of America in 2000 by Abbeville Press,
22 Cortlandt Street, New York, N.Y. 10007.
First published in Mexico in 1998 by Revimundo, S.A. de C.V.
Copyright © 1998 Revimundo, S.A. de C.V.*

*First edition 10 9 8 7 6 5 4 3 2 1
Library of Congress Catalog Card Number: 99-65297
ISBN 0-7892-0621-8*

Acknowledgments:

ING. MARCO ANGUIANO • CONNIE ACERO GUTIÉRREZ • GRACE ACERO (PHOENIX, AZ.) • BRÍGIDO ALVARADO JÁUREGUI • ABRAHAM ALVARADO JÁUREGUI • BRÍGIDO ALVARADO TORRES • LIC. AGUSTÍN BARRIOS GÓMEZ • LIC. CARLOS BERNAL • MARCO BUENINCK • ING. PEDRO BLAKE OLIVARES • MA. LUISA BETANCOURT GÓMEZ P. • ISABEL CAMARGO • IAN CHADWICK (http://www.georgian.net/rally/tequila/index.html) • ING. SERGIO CORREU GLEAVES • FEDERICO CATALANO • GUSTAVO CISNEROS GARCÍA • ING. FELIPE CAMARENA OROZCO • ING. CARLOS C. CAMARENA CURIEL • ING. FELIPE CAMARENA CURIEL • LIC. CARLOS CARRILLO • SRA. PATRICIA CARRILLO • LIC. SONIA ESPÍNDOLA DE LA LLAVE • SIGFRIDO ESCALANTE • ROXANA ESCALANTE • JENNIKATE ESTAVILLO • NIDIA ESQUIVEL DE GALÁN • LUCILLA FLORES DE CLAVÉ • FERNANDO GONZÁLEZ DE ANDA • FERNANDO GONZÁLEZ • LUZ MARÍA GONZÁLEZ • MARTÍN- JON GARCÍA URTIAGA • JULIO GONZÁLEZ ESTRADA • FRANCISCO J. GONZÁLEZ G. • LAURA GARCÍA DE ALBA • LIC. ANTONIO GUERRA AUTREY • MANUEL GUTIÉRREZ DELGADO • JESÚS HERNÁNDEZ • JUAN HERNÁNDEZ • LIC. PATRICIA IBARRA • PEDRO JUÁREZ • GRACIELA DE LA VEGA • JOSÉ LUIS FCO. LÓPEZ • MANUEL LÓPEZ GARIBAY • JEFF LUCKEROTH (http://pwp.value.net/reroof/tequila/index.html) • CARMEN MARÍNEZ COULSON • FRANCISCO MARTÍNEZ GONZÁLEZ • ENRIQUE MARTÍNEZ GUERRRERO • JORGE MASSÚ • ENRIQUE MÉNDEZ RUIZ • ORIOL MESTRE • LIC. IVALÚ MIRELES ESPARZA • PAUL PACULT (http://www.spiritjournal.com/) • LIC. JÓSE LUIS PANTOJA PÉREZ • ING. JUAN CARLOS PIÑA TINAJERO • CARLOS PÉREZ • LEONARDO RODRÍGUEZ MORENO • FRANCISCO JAVIER ROMERO DUARTE • ING. SALVADOR ROSALES TORRES • VÍCTOR MANUEL ROSALES • FLOR RUVALCABA • ING. JAVIER SALGADO • LIC. HÉCTOR SÁNCHEZ CUEVAS • MARCO SANTA CRUZ • SILVIA SAUZA GUTIÉRREZ • JOSÉ FRANCISCO TORRES LANDA • JOSÉ GUADALUPE TORRES LÓPEZ • ING. MOISÉS TAVARES • LIC. RAMÓN VALDEZ GONZÁLEZ • BRIAN WEINER • RALPH WIDEMAN • ING. LUIS YERENAS RUVALCABA

TEQUILA

The spirit of Mexico

Tequila

The spirit of Mexico

TEQUILA
The spirit of Mexico

Preface
CARLOS MONSIVÁIS

Photography
MICHAEL CALDERWOOD

Text
ENRIQUE MARTÍNEZ LIMÓN

Abbeville Press Publishers

New York • London

Contents

Preface
Tequila with lime and other table talk

There are two ways of looking at it. Neither one is wrong; in fact, they complement each other. There is tequila, the oil that greases the wheels of machismo and facilitates mind-numbing sprees; and tequila, the connoisseur's drink, delight that leads to gastronomic pleasures and choice of the discerning palate. At the heart of this paradox lies a century of fast- and slow-changing habits and customs, a century of dynamic and organized change, a century of triumphal gaiety as well as of institutionalized criticism of machismo. To follow the evolution of tequila drinking is to follow, albeit indirectly, the transformation of a number of different rituals: the ritual of mealtimes, the ritual of unquestionable valor, the ritual of virile camaraderie, the ritual of the affairs of the night and that of the trials of the throat.

According to Enrique Martínez Limón's excellent text, tequila has been distilled in Mexico for the past four hundred years. It takes its name, which means "stone that cuts," from a former village, now a city, in the state of Jalisco, whose climate ranges from temperate to fiercely hot. In the beginning, tequila was processed from the blue, green, or ash-colored agaves as well as from local mescals with evocative names such as Azul Rayado, Siggüin, Criollo, Pata de Mula, Moraleño, Chato, Mano Larga, Bermejo, Zahuayo, and Zopilote. Toward the end of the nineteenth century, mescal or tequila began its fifteen minutes of fame, which now appears to stretch indefinitely into the future. In 1902 or 1903 a German botanist, Herr Weber, who dedicated himself to the study of different varieties of agave, registered the family of *Agave tequilana azul* in the taxonomy of succulents. Later and for much the same reason that the cartographer Amerigo Vespucci's name was irrevocably lent to that of the New World, this agave came to be known as *Agave tequilana Weber azul* (though with perhaps fewer repercussions than in the case of Amerigo). According to Martínez Limón, both the campesinos and the locals refer to the *Weber* as a mescal.

Tequila's rise to fame, from humble origins in the years of the dictatorship of Porfirio Díaz, followed the course and fate of the Mexican Revolution. In the stories, novels, testimonials, and photographs of the time, tequila is the spark and glow of the rifle and the gun; "If I am to be killed tomorrow, I had better enjoy a drink today." In the words of the wounded lover of La Valentina,

"If you don't like me drinking tequila, tomorrow I'll drink sherry
If you don't like seeing me drunk, tomorrow I'll make sure you won't see me."

The aura of romance given to the Revolution by the governments that attributed to it their legitimacy should not blind us to the overriding facts: weeks, months, and years of exhaustion and physical horror, violent captures of towns and cities followed by compensatory orgies, barbarities committed by the masses that were a delayed imitation of those committed by their rulers. The ideals that were achieved should be placed in the context of the cruel reality of these events, including the alcoholism that the war engendered, a brutish habit of those already brutalized by exploitation, masters and servants alike. However, as befits an allegory tailored to suit the whims of the majority, the toasts raised to the revolution and its mythical 1 million dead are never with champagne but with tequila. Because of its geographical origins, the social roots of many of the fighting men, the prestige or otherwise that the drink has acquired, and its amazing ability to incite a riot of the senses, tequila has become the liquid symbol of a people in arms. At times of exaltation or catastrophe, of celebration of the life force or mortal combat against the tedium of those condemned to a tragic end, of happy or unfortunate love affairs, people make use of a variety of stimulants, and in Mexico first amongst them is tequila.

Although difficult to prove, it is not an exaggeration to say that the Mexican Revolution with its mountainous tangle of myths and realities has placed tequila fatally hand in hand with courage, with the ecstasy of staying alive, with the desperation and frustration of the fighter and those who unwittingly suffer the consequences of war. Yet this label of "the drink of the trenches" is what has helped launch tequila along the path of industrialization. Pulque still remains the inevitable drink of the campesino, and hot evening parties demand beer. But in the mythical world of the cartridge belt and thick mustachios, of flashing eyes, the wide sombrero, and shouts of "Viva Mexico, sons of ...!" it is tequila that is revered by the fearless and avoided by the gutless.

What a curious destiny for a drink: the qualities of tequila have now made it a defining characteristic of the nation at play. And this is despite the wealth of real and legendary consequences attributed to the drink: the excitation that challenges the world, the jubilation and irrationality that go hand in hand, and the fluctuating mists of incomprehension. What happens is both simple and complex. Because of its celebratory virtues as well as the storms it can raise, tequila acts as regulator for the parade of delicacies that adorn both the epic and the mundane Mexican banquet table. In the process, tequila is vividly linked to the Mexican's peak of excess—the moment when, emboldened by physical courage, bent on self-destruction, and given to unruly behavior, he becomes a creator of great institutions and an inventor of popular cultures, producing a repertoire of unique characters, appetites, and exaggerations. The revolutionary wipes his lips on his shirt, the soldier raises his glass to his ideals, the newcomer to the big-city bar is encouraged to recount his tales from the country tavern, the campesino in his barn lifts his glass to ward off drought or hurricanes. This is the stuff of legends as well as of real life, and for better or for worse all is laid at the door of tequila.

"Who in this life is not familiar / with the well-known betrayal / that follows a sad love affair; / who does not then go to a bar, / demanding a tequila and demanding a song?"

The extraordinary popular urban culture generated in Mexico between the 1930s and the 1950s took full advantage of some of the lessons learned during the revolution, among them the questionable but persuasive idea summed up by the poet William Blake: "The path of excess leads to the palace of wisdom." The entertainment industry, including cinema, records, radio, vaudeville theater, and cabarets, dedicated much space and time to tequila. This was the great moment of Mexican nationalism, and in both natural and induced ways as many emblems and signals of national identity as possible were sought to parade.

From the decade of the 1930s onward, *ranchero* comedy and melodrama saw in tequila an image of great significance: fiesta, pain, laughter, the smiles that eternally accompany tears, sorrow, fellowship, the happiness that explodes in desperate acts, the joy of the palate. It was sufficient to show a bottle on the table and the little glass full beside it for faces to light up immediately.

Cinema was in urgent need of new institutional icons to inspire both comedy and drama. Directors and scriptwriters alike turned to images of the mariachi, the betrayed man, the community in search of festivity, the agonized outpouring of secrets, the metamorphosis of the peaceful man into a hurricane of fury, the fierce *macho* dissolving in tears. To carry the imagination along such rough yet delectable roads, a strong drink was called for. Film belonged to the masses; only rarely were attributes of the middle classes accepted or tolerated, and then only to make fun of them. This was the great claim of tequila.

Remember the great composer José Alfredo Jiménez who enthroned tequila in the eternal night of existential revelations? "Go for it, my friend, and don't hold back." There is no doubt that he was responsible for taking the celebratory genre of drunkenness to its peak, as well as to its eventual obsolescence. The times and the composer have outlasted his explicit ideology. From this distance we can appreciate the purpose of the songs of this anti-epic partygoer: to force the listener to experience some kind of immediate, intense emotion. Master of ceremonies of all those profound feelings triggered by sentimentality, José Alfredo placed tequila at the forefront of spiritual commitments. What other drink eliminates the need for further explanation and imprints "Mexican-ness" on any scene?

*"I wanted to forget
the way they do in Jalisco,
but those mariachis and the tequila
Only made me cry."*

Now that we have established the central role played by tequila ("the spirit of Mexico"), it is time to look at the dimensions of its industry and its most famous brands: Sauza, Cuervo, Herradura, Orendain, 7 Leguas, and hundreds of others. Their success has been phenomenal, and throughout the world people with no thought of curing their spiritual ailments are now drinking tequila as an aperitif. Specialists or connoisseurs—who might also be called "agavologists"—are appearing. The tequila is the same, it just fulfills other needs. Witness the difference between "bottoms up, pal" and "savor the flavor." Today we have the sophistications of the lime-and-salt routine, the scientific or quasi-scientific appreciation of the drink's qualities, the techniques of the expert, the descriptions distinguishing a "young" tequila from rested, aged, or white ("silver") tequila, the critical interpretations of different palates, technical precautions against hangovers, and a universe of professional tequila tasters—all powerful indications of a remarkable change in perception.

Without a doubt tequila is the people's drink of Mexico, but it has also now become popular with the rest of the world. It is to be found on the tables of all social classes. The present-day mythology behind tequila lies essentially in its flavor and in the pronouncements of its connoisseurs, in the immediate pleasure of its taste and not in the situations to which it might give rise. The tequila industry is a proud one. Tequila is specifically a Mexican product (as the certification process now dictates). Unfettered by the past, it provides the whole world with the opportunity to say, "Salud!" Tequila's long journey continues, with all the pleasures and risks involved. It is now the aficionado rather than the national temperament to whom the future belongs.

CARLOS MONSIVÁIS

Introduction

Tequila? I don't think so! Since when has tequila been a beverage for people like me? Everyone knows that tequila is lowbrow, fine for poor peons, longshoremen, wrestlers, eclectic writers, painters who charge by the square yard, and low-life lawyers. Everyone knows that tequila is too strong, even dangerous, and that it makes you falling-down drunk. They say it was invented for thieves and murderers, because it drives men mad. Tequila is not a class act. Period! How can I possibly offer tequila to my guests? I'll serve them whiskey, brandy, vodka, cognac—anything intended for educated people with good taste— but tequila? I don't think so!

Shocking as it may seem, educated people with good taste are drinking tequila everywhere—in Mexico and at least fifty other countries. In the United States it's adored and revered. In Europe it rubs shoulders with the nobility, graces the tables of ancient monarchies, and has won the hearts of musicians, filmmakers, and poets alike.

From Tierra del Fuego to the land of the Eskimos the Americas have opened their arms to

tequila. And though literate youths in Hong Kong may not know if Mexico

is a mile away from Toronto, they do know that the tequila they drink with relish comes

from that faraway, mythical place called Mexico.

Suddenly, we hear talk of the tequila boom. *Boom* means "to resound, thunder, bellow,

or roar." It also means "apex, prosperity, and fast development." In Mexico, tequila has

been made for 400 years, but only now, at the end of the twentieth century, has it

caught the world's attention. Thousands of people, from rustic peasants to powerful

business leaders, have managed to convince the world that tequila never had a pact with

the devil and that it is, on the contrary, a genuine gift from the gods. Some even say it

promises an intimate moment in the dark corner of a cantina.

Tequila is known by many names—agave firewater, cactus juice, mescal wine,

liquid fury, divine pleasure.

So, let's not hold back. Let's talk tequila. Let the god Ome Tochtli, his mother

Mayahuel, and the 400 rabbits of agave[2] tell their story to our people and the world.

Tequila, the spirit of Mexico, has arrived.

Above: *The agave fields of tequila are accessible by dirt tracks, some of which were laid down centuries ago to connect the villages in the area.*

Page 18: *Casasola Archive (INAH photographic collection)*

De Cocula es el mariachi,
de Tecalitlán, los sones,
de San Pedro, su cantar,
de Tequila, su mezcal...[1]

Tequila country:
where and how it is grown

 Magueys • In the Antillean language, *maguey* was the name the natives had for what we now call the century plant (or aloe). When the Spaniards arrived and started cataloging the vegetation they found, from California to Venezuela, they extended this name to cover 400 varieties of these spiny plants. Predominant among them was a kind of pineapple with fleshy branches whose slim cattail arms grow sometimes straight and sometimes in a whimsical, folded fashion. When they are mature some of these plants are three times taller than a man, while others view the world from the height of a youth or child. The flowering stems can reach a height of up to 40 feet (12 m), and the leaves' colors vary from a soft green to purple, passing through various blue tones, with or without yellow bands of varying width.

From time immemorial, pre-Hispanic American peoples cultivated the maguey for its fibers as well as many other parts of the plant. They used the sap as a beverage, since these succulent plants contain unusually sweet, nutritious juices. Approximately 70 percent of Mexico's territory has an arid or semi desert climate in which 136 different species, 26 subspecies, and 29 varieties of maguey flourish. These include the small henequens, whose fibers were traditionally used by the ancient Central Americans to make clothes and household utensils, and the great magueys that grow in the central plateau and sometimes reach a height of more than 10 feet (3 m) and a width of 30 (10m). During the middle of the eighteenth century the great Swedish botanist and natural historian Carolus Linnaeus catalogued the magueys as "agaves" or "agavaceas," almost certainly because he found their aesthetic forms "illustrious"—*agavus* in Latin.[3]

Many people think agaves are desert plants, and because of this they refer to them as cacti.

Certainly agaves have much in common with cacti: a succulent mass, similar vascular systems, and superficial textures that are alike; both have thorns and are able to survive in extreme climates and poor soil. However, for botanists the distinctions are great. Agaves are monocotyledonous plants (with indivisible seeds, like corn), while the cacti are dicotyledonous (like beans and legumes, which can easily be divided into two halves). The agave is not a cactus. When one reads that tequila is "cactus juice," the writer has not done his homework.

Pulque · The ancient Mexicans used various techniques to obtain juice from the maguey plant. For example, they cut into its heart and scraped it while the plant was still alive. The accumulated juices were crystalline and viscous, sweet, and slightly astringent. The Spaniards called this liquid *aguamiel* (honey water). When this juice is fresh it is a nourishing drink, but in a few hours it begins to ferment, acquiring a milky white color and developing an alcoholic content. In this second stage it is known as pulque, and it works as a tonic. However, like any alcoholic beverage, it can cause inebriation.

For at least three hundred years, pulque has been the traditional drink of Mexico. Magueys grow in many areas of the country, but the richest of them are found in the central plateau and its surroundings. Proverbially the state of Hidalgo, especially the region of Apan, produces the best pulque, but that from the state of Mexico is also very good.

Above: The extraction of maguey juice for processing into pulque. Nineteenth-century engraving of C. Linati.

Page 22: "From Cocula, the mariachis, from Tecalitlán, the dances, from San Pedro, the singing, from Tequila, the mescal …" [1]

# of good times and flowing pulque."

Pulque continues to be a popular Mexican drink. There are still many taverns, known as *pulquerías*, in Mexico City and in the states that border the Federal District and the state of Mexico. These *pulquerías* are picturesque places where Mexicans meet because of their cultural bonds or to indulge the nostalgia they still feel for the god Mayahuel.

Although the homemade variety continues to be enjoyed by many families, the pulque industry itself has lost ground to the growing popularity of beer. It has failed to modernize, and without fresh capital it has not been able to invest in the technology needed to develop a process that satisfies the more stringent hygiene requirements.

Mescal • To obtain the juice from certain maguey plants, one needs to do more than just scrape the plant's heart. The ancient inhabitants of Central America discovered that when the hearts of the magueys were cooked in underground ovens, they produced an extraordinary sweet juice that, once fermented, had inebriating qualities. An ancient legend explains:

A great thunderbolt struck a maguey and tore out the plant's heart, setting it alight. Astonished, men saw an aromatic nectar appearing deep inside. They drank it with fear and reverence, accepting it as a gift from the gods.

A more down-to-earth version relates that indigenous farmers used to discard the remains of the plants in large pits where they would rot and later be used as fertilizer. At some point during this period one of the pits caught fire, and the people found the juice from the burned hearts among the remains, thus discovering mescal.

There is no evidence that the ancient Central Americans understood the chemical process of distillation. Their interaction with the maguey was limited to cooking the heart, which they later consumed as a sweet, or mashing and beating it in order to extract the juice. Once it was fermented, they would drink it more as a ritual than for the taste. Knowledge of the distillation process only reached America much later, with the European conquerors.

Measuring degrees of alcohol in the distillery, La Herradura, Amatitán.

At Hacienda Corralejo, in the state of Guanajuato, Charentais stills are used for distillation, a process unique in the tequila industry.

Tequila · The liquid that is produced from the fermented juices of these maguey or agave plants is called mescal. What, then, is tequila? Tequila is the specific type of mescal that is distilled from these unique blue agave plants in the area named Tequila, in the state of Jalisco. From this place the tequila now sold around the world received its name.

Although both the agave and the cactus grow in arid lands, they belong to different botanical families. Mescal cannot be made from cactus juice.

The lands of tequila and blue agave • The word *tequio*, of uncertain origin, means "work, labor, task." Perhaps the word *tequila* refers to a place that was worked or where people worked. Other versions maintain that it comes from the people who lived along the hills and skirts of the Tequilán volcano, where the ethnic group called *tequiltecas*, *tecuilos,* or *tequilinos* prospered.

In the town of Tequila, in the state of Jalisco, all the inhabitants now seem to be experts on history and tradition. They explain that the name of their town and its eponymous beverage is related to a flat stone called obsidian that is common there. Obsidian is a volcanic rock that when polished becomes iridescent. The people of this area say that *tequila* means "stone that cuts," because the edges of obsidian are very sharp, and like them, tequila "cuts" through the throat of those who drink it.

Tequila itself lies 4,260 feet (1,300 m) above sea level and has a temperate and often hot climate. Because of this, wild agave plants abound. Among these agaves one type predominates, carpeting the land in blue. It grows against a background of intense evergreens and juniper trees, which thrive in this area. There are also green agaves dotted with ocher tones, which often have a characteristic ashlike color. For a long time these blue agaves *(zapupes)* were used to produce the "mescal wine" from Tequila. Rarer varieties were called by such colorful names as blue streak, creole, mule's hoof, flat nose, big hand, and buzzard, but today these represent only 1 percent of the total.

Around 1896 Franz Weber, a German naturalist, came to Mexico to study the flora in the eastern part of the country. He became acquainted with a family in Tequila who owned the largest distillery in the area. Their agave plants caught his interest, and through his research one form of the most abundant variety, *Agave tequilana azul*, became the plant of choice. In 1902 or 1903 it was renamed *Agave tequilana Weber azul* in his honor.

Above: *Some of the many types of agave (El Moraleño, Espadín de Oaxaca, Siggüin, Bermejo, Zopilote, and Bacanora) used in the processing of mescal.*

Opposite: *Tequila only comes from Agave tequilana Weber azul.*

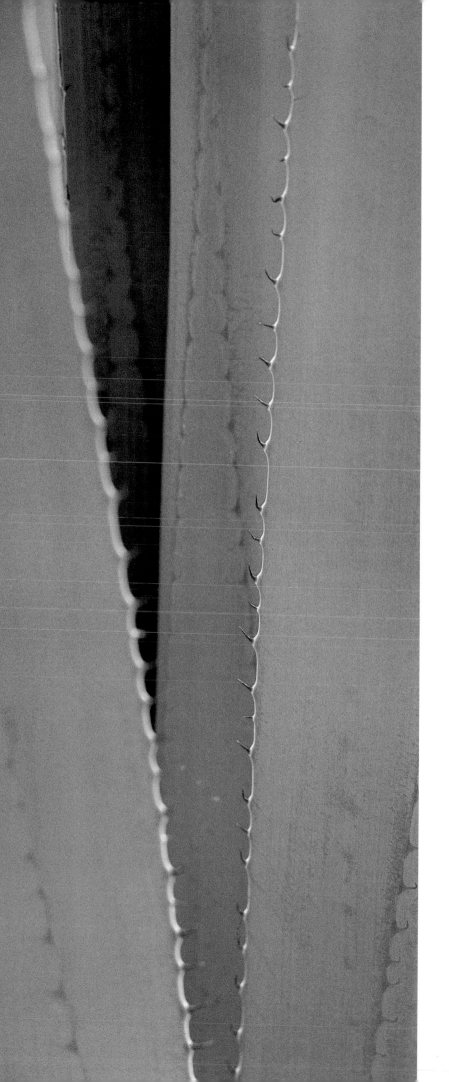

Jalisco cultivates more than 50,000 hectares of *Agave tequilana Weber azul*, but it also occurs to a lesser extent in Michoacan, Nayarit, Guanajuato, and Tamaulipas. In the first two, there are no tequila distilleries. Guanajuato has one distillery in Corralejo (the birthplace of Padre Hidalgo, father of Mexico's Independence) and Tamaulipas another. Today, the state of Jalisco is responsible for 98 percent of tequila production. Of this, 90 percent comes from the regions of Amatitán, Arandas, Atotonilco, El Arenal, Tepatitlán, and Tequila. Eight percent corresponds to the municipalities to the south of Jalisco (principally Ixtlahuacán del Río, Jocotepec, Tlajomulco, Tonaya, and Venustiano Carranza). The remaining 2 percent comes from the aforementioned states of Tamaulipas and Guanajuato.

Overleaf: *Dawn in the colonial town of Tequila: rural, traditional, and mostly peaceful.*

"With love and firewate

What about the worm? • There is a butterfly that, in its larval or pupal stage, can live in the *espadín*, a Oaxacan agave. Long ago someone discovered that these maguey worms were a delicious and nutritious food. To this very day people still eat them roasted or fried. They are also sometimes dried and pulverized and then mixed with salt and spices to make a "worm salt"; mescal drinkers love to add this salt to their drink. One day, some manufacturer decided to insert a worm into the bottle. The idea was that a worm, as a living being, would devour any evil spirit hidden within the mescal. It was also a good way of giving the product an intriguing stamp of origin. Visitors from abroad are fascinated by this worm phenomenon, especially by the aphrodisiac attributes that the worm has now acquired. Mescal drinkers—especially those living outside Mexico—have created an unusual ritual: they eat the worm after finishing up the bottle.

As tequila is itself a mescal, it is understandable that there is great confusion between mescals that have worms and those, like tequila, that don't.

Without a doubt, tequila is a type of mescal. But not all mescals are from Tequila. Some of the mescals from Oaxaca have their own peculiar trademark: the maguey worm.

nothing can hurt you"

Tequila's first cousins • Bacanora • In the northeast of Mexico there is a plant called *Agave potatorum* or *Agave yaquiana* from which a mescal is produced that has been given its very own name: *bacanora*. This is made in Sonora using the traditional method of cooking the agave in subterranean ovens. With *bacanora,* the processes of grinding or pounding, distillation, and aging are unique and differ substantially from those used to make tequila.

While tequila has overcome its black reputation as an aggressive beverage, bacanora still inspires fear even among the people of Sonora. Though the production of this drink has a long history, it became a legal substance in 1992, and now that it is becoming known, those who produce it have bettered the product. Today, significant quantities of bacanora are exported to the United States, and most of it is still made in clandestine distilleries tolerated by the local authorities.

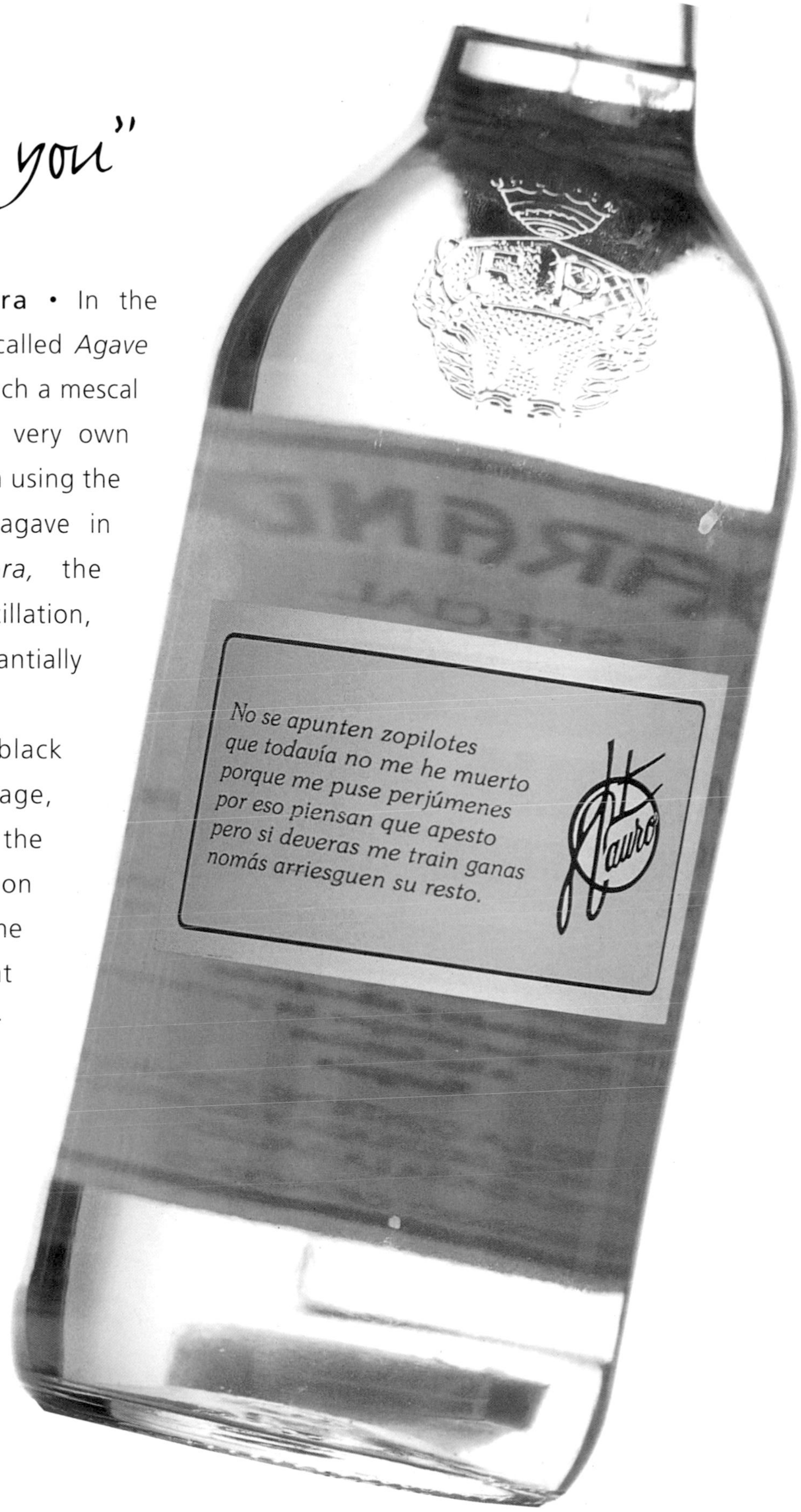

No se apunten zopilotes
que todavía no me he muerto
porque me puse perjúmenes
por eso piensan que apesto
pero si deveras me train ganas
nomás arriesguen su resto.

Charanda, *a cane spirit from the state of Michoacán, is identified by a piece of sugarcane placed in the bottom of the bottle.*

In Sayula, in the state of Jalisco, people say that there is a spirit in purgatory who is known popularly as the Anima

(Spook) de Sayula. They say that this phantom scares the living. One sure way of seeing the ghost is to violate the

local laws of Sayula's mescal. One is supposed to stir the mescal with a piece of rope made from a variety of agave

called lechugilla and then turn it around in circles. If the drinker turns the rope twice, he has a right to two drinks;

if he turns it three times, then it is three drinks, etc. However, if the drinker drinks more than the circles

accomplished, he is "lost," and the spook immediately appears.   From the popular legend of The Spook of Sayula

Blue breast and angel breast • Among tequila's first cousins the most famous, without a doubt, is the mescal that comes from Oaxaca. Produced from a blue agave that grows in the shape of a sword, the mescal is called *pechuga azul* (blue breast) and, in its finest form, *pechuga del ángel* (angel breast). Traditionally it is sold in black earthenware bottles that are lacquered and finely decorated by hand. Now that exports have become so important, these bottles are quite sophisticated. The best mescal that comes from Oaxaca has a soft and agreeable taste. It is up to the drinker's discretion whether to combine it with "worm salt," and some of the bottles actually come with a small bag filled with the condiment.

Rows of agaves often serve as boundaries between the cornfields in the valley of Oaxaca.

Agaves are hermaphroditic plants whose offspring sprout from the bottom of the plant. The stems of the agave are called "quiotes," and their flowering signals the death of the plant.

The mescal called *raicilla* • Along the coast and in the hills of Jalisco, and in eastern Michoacan, farmers produce *raicilla*, a mescal made in a clay pot that is famous for being the strongest of all. The people from Jalisco say that you can drink "one or two drinks and no more" because of its power to inebriate. It is difficult to find and does not appear in government statistics because most of it is produced clandestinely. However, it became well known when a Mexican cartoonist, Ríus, created the character of a distracted philosopher who was only inspired when under the influence of his *raicilla*.

The life and death of the blue agave · Tequila producers know that the blue agave will yield the most tequila if the heart is large. To achieve this result, the farmer must prune the plant so that the heart benefits from as many nutrients as possible. This generally occurs at the end of March or before the first rains. As soon as the stem (or *quiote*) appears, it must be cut out. If it is left uncut, the plant will only be useful for industrial processing. Once the stem is removed, the heart will continue to grow and the plant will live for one more year.

In order to take advantage of the rains, fertilizer is applied to the fields during the month of July. If solid chemical fertilizers are used, each plant manually receives 2.7 to 3.5 ounces (70–100 g) of urea or 28 ounces (800 g) of ammonia sulfate. Another option is to use natural fertilizers, which enrich the soil and make fertilization necessary only every other year.

When the rainy season ends, the crop is weeded, which has the added advantage of avoiding fires that can occur during the dry season.

Thinking ahead • Don Julio González, of the Tres Magueyes company, is a doyen in the tequila industry and a well-known businessman in the region of Atotonilco, Jalisco. He showed us the extensive lands where his company cultivates *Agave tequilana Weber azul*. He told us that the most important part of his work was thinking ahead.

He was referring, of course, to the planting, cultivating, and replanting of mescals (the name that, confusingly, everyone in tequila country gives to these agave plants). Young shoots have to be selectively separated from the older plants so that they do not compete for nutrients, and the most important thing, he insists, is to keep populating the fields with these younger plants, for future production.

Under the expert gaze of Don Julio, his workers select those shoots that have a heart at least the size of a mature orange or grapefruit. Once selected, they are left alone to see if they will prosper. If all goes well, the mother plants are then removed. The fields are first prepared, and the new mescals are placed just beneath the surface in wide, well-separated rows, leaving about 3 feet (1 m) between each plant. The exact placement makes a great deal of difference in the final result.

For the blue agave and its cousins, death occurs 12 to 36 months after its reproduction; that is, after the flowering stem of the plant develops and sprouts. It dies after a kind of senility sets in; the plant grows dry, then rots and goes back into the earth to feed its young.

Above: *"My first tequila factory was a failure," says Don Julio González, today one of the most successful tequila producers. "Processing tequila is not an easy thing, requiring expertise, perseverance, and a lot of hard work."*

Preceding spread: *The laborer who harvests the agaves in the fields of Jalisco is called a jimador. More than a harvest, the cutting process resembles some kind of ferocious hand-to-hand combat, with no quarter given or received.*

"she said to me, 'Turn at the corner, we'll go to my house; after a couple of tequilas we'll see what happens.'"

From the song "Historia del Taxi" by Ricardo Arjona

"Many years ago I broke with the tradition of planting the mescals on top of one another," Don Julio

told us. "It was thought that more mescals meant greater yield. They said I was crazy when they saw

me separating the rows by more than ten feet and then planting out each mescal at three-foot intervals.

The most important factor in the growth of the mescal is sunshine. Should one overshadow another,

they don't develop equally. Planted too closely together, they fight for possession of the earth. I guess I

wasn't that crazy after all: now everybody is doing the same thing!"

Preceding page: The heart of the mescal is called a "pineapple" and can weigh up to 220 pounds (100 kg).

Right: *The principal tool used for harvesting is a coa or hoe. A good jimador or harvester takes 75 seconds to strip the leaves from the mescal.*

The harvest • Although tradition dictates that the mescal harvest should occur in the plant's eighth or ninth year of life, this can vary. Some experts choose to evaluate the condition of the plant rather than measure it by age. Factories may start processing when it is only five years old, despite the fact that the hearts are small and lacking in sugars, limiting the final yield.

The mescal harvest is called *jima* or *jimado*. When the mescal is ready to be processed, the *jimadores* go to the fields armed with various tools, including a *coa*, a kind of steel-tipped hoe that is extremely sharp. Generally, this work occurs in the early hours of the morning or at dusk, and although it appears easy, it actually takes great strength. The harvest may take place at any time of the year, depending on the climate, the humidity, and the maturity of the mescal plant. The training of *jimador* workers is ancestral, as with all people who participate in the productive chain of tequila making. The tequila industry as we know it is already 230 years old, and the history of mescal production even longer.

Sometimes during the harvesting there are accidents. For example, one of the *jimadores* who allowed us to observe his work in a field close to Tequila slipped and drove an agave spine into his hand. Instantly, he took his hoe and cut another one, which he twisted so that its juice fell into the wound. As he later explained it, *"It hurts like hell, because the spine is so sharp that it doesn't stop until it hits the bone, and the bad thing is that it paralyzes your hand. To cure it you use the juice of another spine of the same mescal, and this kills the pain and brings the hand to life quickly so that, in just a few minutes, you can use it again as if nothing had happened. This juice helps any kind of cut, and they tell me it cleans the wound and reduces scars."*

This might sound like an exotic folktale, but the truth is, the *jimador* was back at work ten minutes later!

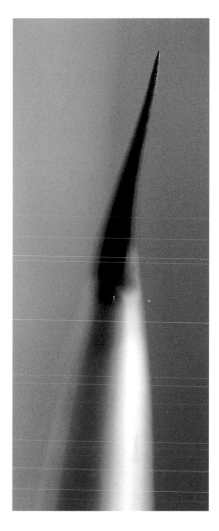

Making Tequila:
a trip through the distilleries

 Cooking • The ancient production of mescal required the cooking of agave hearts in an underground oven. A hole was dug in the earth and filled with wood, then a layer of stones was placed over the hole. The wood was left to burn until the stones and the earth burned like coals. Then the agave hearts were placed inside, within layers of humid fodder. Next the oven was sealed and dirt thrown upon it. A small opening was left so that the fire could breathe and the cook could tell what was happening inside by the odors released by the vapors. This process is called the *tatemado* of the mescal. The cooking lasted one or two days at least, followed by another day or two while the oven was allowed to cool and the plant's sugars hydrolyze. During the *tatemado* the agave juices soaked up some of the wood's aroma.

Since 1850, producers have abandoned *tatemado* in tequila production, although a few isolated distilleries in some areas of Jalisco were still using it in the early 1920s. Today, this procedure has been modified and is done with steam.

Traditionally, depending on the oven's size, the steam cooking lasts 24 to 36 hours. The temperature remains at 175 to 200°F (80 to 95°C) until the moment when the vapor becomes fierce and forces itself through the holes. Then the oven is turned down. The operation has to be programmed, taking into account the distillery's capacity for grinding and storing the must and distilling the cooked mescal. Small distilleries may possess only one oven, while the larger ones may have up to twenty working nonstop.

When large quantities of tequila are being produced on a daily basis, the ovens frequently cannot keep up with the production that precedes cooking. Consequently, some distilleries have begun to use huge pressure cookers (autoclaves) to increase their efficiency. When the

cooking and cooling process is finished, the bits of mescal look very different. The white pulp, though still fibrous, now has a brown-orange color. An ax is no longer needed to break it, and it shreds easily in one's hands. In its raw stage it is bitter and has practically no odor. In this new stage it has a sweet, agreeable smell and has been transformed into an exquisite candy.

Page 48: *White oak barrels used for the aging of tequila in the La Herradura cellars. The seals covering the corks guarantee a minimum twelve-month aging period.*

The basic process for producing any mescal, including tequila, is a combination of the following steps: cooking, grinding or beating, fermentation, filtration, and distillation.

Facing page, left: *Ovens sealed with adobe to begin the cooking process, Hacienda Corralejo, Guanajuato.*
Right, top: *Blue agave "pineapples" recently harvested.*
Middle: *The cut "pineapple" before cooking.*
Bottom: *The cooked "pineapple" before crushing.*

Near left: *Ovens and cooked agave on the production line at La Herradura.*

Grinding and beating · Many years ago, the cooked

mescal was beaten with sticks or the blunt sides of axes. Later a flour mill was used, modified by the introduction of a round pit over which a large, circular stone was turned by mules and other beasts of burden. In front of this grinding stone, the cooked agave "pineapples" were stirred by hand with a two- or three-pronged hoe or spade. This method crushed and pressed out the juice, slackening or shredding the fibers that immediately reabsorbed most of the juice.

In order to recover the liquid, the workers filled large wooden barrels with the mixture, then carried them on their heads to the fermentation vats. Inside these vats a practically naked worker known as the beater would stand or float in the mixture of juices and mescal fibers. The beater stirred or "washed" the fibers by separating them with his hands and feet, helping the mixture liquefy. Under the liquid was a brown mass taking up a

*The cooked agaves are crushed in a mill. At El Centenario, the 7 Leguas tequila factory (**left**), horses are used to turn the 3-ton stone wheel, while in the new Seagram's factory (**above**) another type of horsepower is preferred.*

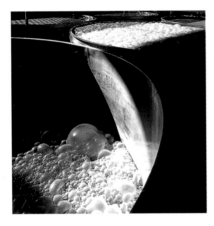

quarter of the space, and the rest, the valuable mescal juices, were then transferred to large fermentation vats.

Steam and later electricity have increased efficiency in tequila production. In recent years the sugarcane industry has also improved its grinding systems. The tequila plants now have shredding mills, very similar to those used for sugarcane.

Fermentation • Today, the "wash" of the fibers is mechanical. The residue is removed so that the fermentation vat contains only liquid, either juice or the washed water (there is now rarely a man immersed in the mixture). Some distilleries combine the two steps: first the liquid is separated and put in the fermentation vat, then some of the fiber residue is added to lend a touch of tradition.

What happens inside the tank? • If the mescal juices are allowed to rest in the vat with the residue from the agave's skin, the biological interaction of the bacteria and yeast will consume the sugars and change them into a variety of byproducts, such as ethyl alcohol and methanol.

If the atmospheric temperature is warm—say between 68 and 86°F (20 and 30°C)—the natural fermentation process will last from two to five days. If the climate is cooler, or even cold, the process can last up to twelve days. One way of accelerating the fermentation process is to add natural yeast, principally beer. Chemical catalyzers like urea and some sulfates are also used, since they work as sources of nitrogen (nitrites or nitrates). Some old tequila masters think that using yeast as an additive is a sin, and that using urea or sulfates is tantamount to destroying the character of the tequila.

The raw materials used at this stage of production determine the differences between the relative purity and quality of the tequilas. Although official requirements demand that the producers use at least 51 percent *Agave tequilana Weber azul,* the government does allow the producers to do whatever they want with the remaining 49 percent.

They have to find sources of sugars that suit them best in cost, supply, and quality. There are, of course, many factories in which the tequila produced contains 100 percent agave, but where this is not the case, the balance of the liquid is usually made up with cane spirit, produced in large quantities in Jalisco as well as other parts of the country.

Traditionally, one of the workers will plunge into the tank to stir the must with his body and thus encourage the fermentation process.
It is said that this leaves his skin as "soft as a baby's bottom".

Distillation hall with copper stills in La Rojeña, manufacturer of José Cuervo tequila.

Pouring of the must into the still,
the traditional way in La Alteña
(facing page),
and the industrialized version in the
Seagram's factory
(this page).

Filtration • When the tequila must is ready for distillation, it is necessary to filter it and eliminate the solid fiber residues as well as other impurities. Filtration is a process that has been used for centuries, and modern factories achieve it with great efficiency.

Once filtered, the musts furnished to the distilleries or the distillation towers are almost perfect mixtures, containing only a small quantity of suspended particles.

Distillation • Besides water, the filtered must contains aldehyde and ester, some of which will be the source of characteristic flavors and aromas, and in addition ethyl alcohol and other major and minor alcohols. Some of the minor harmful ones such as methanol are a normal byproduct of the fermentation process. To eliminate unwelcome substances a distillation process is needed. This has to be done with care and patience so the end product is not only safe but also ensures that the taste, aroma, and body of the beverage remain intact.

Two retorts were once generally used: a distiller and a rectifier. The first distillation obtains a liquid that is not as yet tequila. It is called "ordinary," and its ethyl alcohol content is about 20 to 30 percent of its volume. This first distillation also produces the so-called head (which contains volatile substances such as aldehyde, ester, and minor alcohols) and the tail (containing mostly water but also some heavier materials). These waste products, which along with the remains of the must are left in vats and retorts, are the dregs that make an inferior drink.

By rectifying the ordinary liquid in the second distillation, the head and tail are separated and removed once more. The principal product of this distillation will be true white tequila, a crystalline liquid with an alcoholic content that varies between 40 and 57 degrees Gay-Lussac (GL; see page 65), at a temperature of approximately 68°F (20°C).

Instead of retorts, some modern factories have opted to use distillation towers, which contain more expensive equipment. It is interesting to note that some small factories with insufficient means to buy retorts or new distillation towers use reconstructed or homemade equipment and still manage to keep abreast of the new tequila boom.

"For all misfortunes, a tequila"

Tequila *Blanco* • The end result of this distillation process is white tequila with an alcoholic content of 55 degrees GL, often called silver in the U.S. With this basic product the preparation for commercial sale begins. In general terms, there are four kinds of pure tequila: *joven* (young), which is sometimes called *abocado* (mild), *blanco* (white), *reposado* (rested), and *añejo* (aged). By calling these tequilas "pure," we mean that they are bottled without being mixed with any liquors, infusions, pieces of fruit, or seeds. Hence they are not liqueurs or creams.

Normally, the tequila that will be pure white is stored in large stainless steel vats. Nevertheless, some factories still use oak vats or barrels, which do not affect the liquid since it is stored in this way for only a brief period of time before the tequila is passed on to the bottlers. If the bottling plant is at the distillery, the tequila is moved to selection tanks that fill the bottles. Here it is diluted with water (nonmineral, distilled, or simply high-quality water, depending on the producers' resources). It then passes through one last filter, and ends in bottles with a gradation of 38 to 46 degrees GL.

In the La Mexicana distillery belonging to the Orendain company there is a 980-square-foot room with a domed roof 60 feet (18 m) high. Here, white tequila is homogenized and stored in gigantic vats. It is difficult to believe that one is surrounded by half a million liters of white tequila. One cannot help but think: what hose can I attach myself to while the guard isn't looking?

Tequila *Joven* • Tequila is called *joven* (young) when it rests for less than 60 days, (often much less). This variety of tequila is usually white and spends a few days in oak vats where certain changes take place, making it *abocado* (mild). In the United States tequila *joven,* referred to as gold, has been a great favorite for many years. Sometimes it is colorless, but most often it has a light golden or amber color because of the immersion in the vat of the *mona,* a bag that contains oak shavings and is placed inside the barrel or cask. This *mona* tints the tequila and even gives it a slight wood flavor. If the color obtained in this way is insufficient, a natural caramel coloring is added. To smooth its flavor, glycerin can be added too. Tequila *joven* is normally 38 to 40 degrees GL.[4]

Tequila *Reposado* · For a tequila to merit the name *reposado* (rested), it has to remain in wooden vats or barrels for 60 days or more. During this time, the wood alters the flavor and slightly modifies the color. Its time of repose may last for months as long as it does not surpass one year; tequila that rests for more than this time is called *añejo* (aged) tequila.

Tequila *reposado* marks a change in consumer patterns. It is smoother than white (*reposados* are usually bottled at 38 degrees GL), and like *joven* has a natural soft gold or clear honey coloring and a taste that preserves the wood flavor without losing the strong mescal essence. Because of this, it has stolen the hearts of tequila drinkers and has become a great favorite both in Mexico and abroad. Most *reposados* are 100 percent agave; the few that are not are required to contain at least 80 percent agave must and 20 percent other sugars.

Tequila *Añejo* · A tequila officially becomes *añejo* (aged) when it has been kept in storage in a new or used oak barrel for over 12 months.[5] During this time, the white tequila color changes considerably. It may be gold, deep amber, or even very dark. Its taste is impregnated with that of the wood, and certain chemical reactions take place. The quality of the wood as well as the age of the barrel are very important to the end result. A new barrel, with its resin untapped, strongly affects the tequila flavor and makes it spicy. An old barrel may make the flavor less intense or even poor. As long as the allotted time frames are honored and the Council for the Regulation of Tequila's seals are placed on all the barrels, the producer can mix different lots together until the correct taste has been achieved. Then the producer can claim to have a unique *añejo* or a new commercial brand.

Its prolonged aging slowly transforms *añejo* into a drink they say is "dressed in tails." Although in professional taster's terms it is inaccurate to refer to cognac or brandy when discussing tequila, these *añejos* carry such prestige that the comparison is often made. Today some companies sell tequila that has been aged for two, three, or even five years and can compete in price and satisfaction with any fine cognac.

100 percent pure? • The purity of tequila, or any mescal, lies in the quality of the must used in the distillation. The official standard, NOM-006-1994, clearly states which substances tequila can and cannot contain. At least 51 percent of tequila's content has to come from the juices of *Agave tequilana Weber azul,* and these agaves have to have been cultivated in Mexico in the states authorized to produce it—Jalisco, Michoacan, Guanajuato, Nayarit, and Tamaulipas. If all of the tequila must comes from those agaves, the producers have to point this out on the label, which should say "100% pure agave" or "100% pure *Agave tequilana Weber azul*."

The standard also fixes strict guidelines on toxic substances. The producer tests his own product, but the Council demands that a sample from each lot be tested at a certified laboratory. Chromatographic tests are made, and no liquid gets the green light until it has been approved by this analysis. If the product is unacceptable, it must be disposed of, or in the best of cases, distilled again. There are many

Page 60: Stainless steel settling tanks in the Sauza tequila factory and wooden versions (page 61) in the José Cuervo installations.

Above: The room where alcohol levels are measured after the distillation process, La Rojeña, Tequila.

Opposite: The scale established by the French scientist Gay-Lussac, for measuring the alcoholic content of a liquid.

Overleaf: Selection of alcoholic drinks manufactured in Europe, now prohibited from using the magic word **tequila** *on their labels.*

substances that are outlawed and others that are tolerated, depending on the level of the substance involved. The most risky is methanol. In a sample of tequila equivalent to 100 milliliters of absolute alcohol, the maximum level of methanol allowed is 300 milligrams. The dry extract from tequila *blanco* should not have a greater solid weight than 1 percent of the sample, and in the case of *reposados* and *añejos* the maximum is 5 percent.

If the beverage does not fulfill these requirements, it cannot be labeled tequila. A product that does not adhere to these regulations is abnormal tequila, an imitation, or even an illegal product. The sale of these false tequilas is not prohibited, but their producers are asked to eliminate the word *tequila* from their labels and use a substitute such as *aguardiente de agave* (agave liquor).

The inebriating substance in all distilled drinks, or the spirit, is ethyl or ethane alcohol, a liquid 96 percent miscible in water. Under normal conditions, the most concentrated ethyl alcohol has at least 4 percent

water in its makeup. The French scientist Gay-Lussac, author of several important studies on the physics of gases, created a scale based on the metric system that is frequently used for measuring the alcoholic content of a beverage. A degree of Gay-Lussac (GL) refers to a mixture that contains 1 percent volume of alcohol at 68°F (20°C). Simply put, just double the degrees GL of alcoholic content to find the "proof" spirit of what you are drinking. If the label on your tequila bottle says 38 degrees GL, it is then 76 proof, quite common for tequila.

In practice, Mexico has defended tequila with the same tenacity with which the French have defended cognac. In the 1950s the Treaty of Lisbon was signed, and since then various initiatives have been enacted to confirm Mexico as tequila's exclusive place of origin. In 1997, after lengthy negotiations, the European Community accepted the following basic premise of entitlement for the origin of tequila: "Tequila is that which the Mexican government claims it to be."

Right: In November 1997 the European Community gave official recognition to Mexico as the place of origin of tequila.

The pioneers · The Spanish captain Cristóbal de Oñate, an official under Nuño de Guzmán, conqueror of Mexico's east coast, founded the Villa of Tequila on April 12, 1530. Oñate also founded the city of Guadalajara.[6]

How did a meeting between a Spaniard who longed for his vineyards and the natives who knew the recipe for fermenting mescal occur? We will never know, but we can guess that it must have happened around 1550 or 1560, when the region was finally at peace. Until this time, the

Above: *Don Pedro Sánchez de Tagle, founder of the first distillery in Tequila, Jalisco.*

Right: *The crushing stone in the old distillery at San José del Refugio, Amatitán.*

warlike inhabitants of the hills and valleys of Jalisco had come close to exterminating the Spanish invaders.

Fifty years later, historical documents clearly refer to mescal, but not to tequila. It might be that the meeting between the Spaniards and the natives did not actually occur in Tequila but nearby, perhaps on the skirts of the volcano, in the Amatitán Valley, or near Tepatitlán, since these were the areas where the blue *zapupe* grew.

The Spaniards or Creoles drank wine or its derivatives imported from their homelands or from local resources, since grapevines had been arriving in New Spain since the seventeenth century. Because of their traditions, the natives drank pulque or fermented maize. When the sugarcane plantations began to proliferate in Mexico (a long time after the Spaniards took sugarcane to Cuba), some were adapted to the production of cane alcohol and rum. For a long time, the Spaniards and Creoles preferred these to the agave distillations.

Above: *Mexico City and surrounding areas. From Vistas, trajes y monumentos, C. Castro, J. Campillo, and G. Rodríguez, (Mexico Library).*

Facing page, top: *Nineteenth-century label from one of the José Cuervo distilleries.*

Facing page, below: *Old flagon used to carry tequila, Sauza Museum.*

Where was mescal wine or tequila wine distilled for the first time? Some say that it was in Amatitán, others that it was in Arenal. No documentation exists to clarify this dispute. We do know that a wealthy landowner from Tequila, Don Pedro Sánchez de Tagle, the marquis of Altamira, gathered up various rustic techniques and created an industry around them. He planted the first agave fields in order to produce mescal wine, and he installed the first distillery in Tequila at the beginning of the eighteenth century.[7]

The Cuervo, Rojas, Gallardo, and Beckman families • In 1795, the concession for producing legitimate mescal wine on a large scale was given to José María Guadalupe Cuervo. In the early 1800s his son José Ignacio Faustino Cuervo and his daughter, María Magdalena Ignacia Cuervo, inherited the Taberna de Cuervo from their father, its founder. María Magdalena married a Vicente Albino Rojas and deeded her inheritance to him.

Rojas was a hardworking man who took charge and expanded the distillery, but also changed its name. The custom among mescal wine producers was to name their taverns or distilleries after their owners; hence the one that Vicente Albino Rojas managed, and later inherited, was called La Rojeña. To this day the factory owned by the Cuervo firm in Tequila, Jalisco, bears this name.[8] One Jesús Flores became the proprietor of La Rojeña in about 1860 and eventually inherited it from the descendants of Vicente Albino Rojas. He gave new momentum to the industry, and his distilleries were the first to bottle tequila in glass jugs. We know that in 1880 he sold almost 700,000 liters of tequila, or an average of almost 2,000 liters a day. Jesús Flores left everything to his second wife, Ana González Rubio, who today is still considered the family matriarch. In 1900 she married José Cuervo Labastida, then the head of La Constancia. This particular José Cuervo, carrying the same name as his ancestors, took control and soon managed to recuperate the fortunes of the family firm. The name reverted to La Rojeña and their tequila bore the label José Cuervo, the name we see in the advertising, on the bottles, and shining down from the billboards that festoon the entrance to the town of Tequila.

Cuervo's official owner was still Ana González Rubio, and in 1934 she willed La Rojeña to her niece Guadalupe Gallardo. José Cuervo continued as head of the firm and continued to expand it until his death in 1921, when the management reverted to his widow, Doña Ana. The inheritor of Cuervo in the following generation was Virginia Gallardo, who married Juan Beckman, a German consul who lived in Guadalajara. Cuervo was then willed to her son Juan Beckman Gallardo, and in turn to his son, Juan Beckman Vidal, who is the firm's president today.

From 1758 to the present the Cuervo family has been a force in the tequila industry, even though it is difficult to prove that blood ties exist between the first Cuervo and the current Mexican proprietors, who are owners of 55 percent of the firm's capital.[9]

The Sauza Family • At the beginning of the nineteenth century, Don José Maria Castañeda founded La Antigua Cruz distillery in Tequila, a factory for mescal wine. Years later, in September of 1873, it was bought by one Cenobio Sauza. La Antigua Cruz was not the first distillery that Cenobio Sauza had owned. Before this he had managed La Gallardeña, which he later bought.[10] In 1888 La Antigua Cruz became La Perseverancia, and it still bears this name.

Under the management of Cenobio Sauza the first recorded exportation of mescal wine from Tequila was made to the United States, in six jugs and three barrels, under the Sauza name.[11] Later La Perseverancia was left in the hands of Eladio Sauza, one of the six children of Don Cenobio. Don Eladio was a businessman with wide interests. Though tequila was a good source of income, it did not interest him much. A photograph shows him toasting a friend with cognac.

In 1943 Francisco Javier Sauza, the eldest son of Eladio and an educated man who had traveled the world, became head of the firm. The great success tequila has enjoyed in Mexico and abroad is due in great part to his imaginative approach. He devoted much time and money to making tequila the flourishing business we see today.

Silvia Sauza and her museum • Doña Silvia Sauza Gutiérrez, the daughter of Don Francisco Javier Sauza de la Mora, is a charming woman. She heads the museum that her father founded in their old family home, which stands in the center square of Tequila, Jalisco. The museum is a testament to the achievements of three generations of the Sauza family. Tequila Sauza no longer belongs to the family, having been bought by an Anglo-Spanish consortium, but Silvia Sauza works at the museum for strictly cultural reasons.

The walls of several rooms in the Sauza museum are covered in pictures that detail the history of tequila. The museum also contains old furniture and small traditional tiles decorated with sayings. In what was once Francisco Javier Sauza's living room, on the wall above the bar, one of these plaques reads, "First, with water. Then without water. And finally, like water."

The museum is a record of the century itself. There are diplomas from world's fairs in which Sauza presented its product, and mysterious labels that read "Tequila brandy" or "Mexican whiskey." God knows what was going on in the minds of Don Cenobio and Don Eladio! One also finds samples of the small pottery bottles that were used before tequila was bottled in glass. And there are prizes, tequila glasses in all shapes and sizes, and painted portraits of the family. Some of these were used on labels and calendars or hung inside the distilleries. One of the original letters in the museum was written by the actor John Wayne to Don Francisco Javier, saying that thanks to tequila he was able to work on a movie for twelve hours, even though he had pneumonia!

The transition to modernity · Tequila was scarce for many years after 1940 because there was simply not enough agave available for industrial production. It is interesting to note that although official standards prohibited tequila production with less than 100 percent agave must, the authorities made an exception to this during World War II, when the demand for all kinds of alcohol, both inside and outside Mexico, was great.

By the end of the 1950s, the large tequila firms had begun to refinance the systematic harvesting of the plant, though they had to wait until the agaves matured. Even so, at the

Left: *17 million agaves are required per year to meet present tequila production goals.*
Here, "pineapples" stacked before processing in La Perseverancia, the Tequila Sauza distillery.

Facing page, top:
After the Mexican Revolution, the Tequila Sauza distilleries returned to exporting part of their production to the United States. Here is an example of the much-appreciated "Mexican Whiskey."

Far left: *Certificate of Merit awarded to Don Cenobio Sauza for his "Mescal Brandy" at the World's Columbian Exposition of 1893, in Chicago.*

beginning of the 1960s many factories had to suspend their work because they lacked raw materials. This produced unemployment and also added to an ongoing problem that had existed since the 1930s, the adulteration of tequila. As a result, in 1963 the authorities in charge of commerce created the "DEN-R-9-1964" law, which authorized tequila producers to use mixed musts with a minimum of 70 percent agave juice, the rest to be made up of other sugars (unrefined sugar and molasses). This allowed the factories to keep on working despite the agave shortage.

By 1970 the shortfall had still not been resolved, so the authorities once more reduced the percentage of agave required, this time to 51 percent. Within a decade annual tequila production, which stood at about 23 million liters in 1970, increased to nearly 60 million liters, partly because of these concessions and partly due to a decisive reduction in the production of the high-end, 100 percent agave tequilas.

"*First, with water. Then without water. And finally, like water.*"

During the last two decades tequila and agave production have varied greatly. Though there has been greater development in both field and factory, disagreements between the people who grow agave and the people who produce tequila continue. For many years the distillers set the price of agave, but only up to a point. When it is scarce the people who control the cultivation of the plant can also control the price. Likewise, they can also control the effects of overproduction by forcing the distillers to buy their surplus.

Markets • During the mid-1800s, after Mexico's independence had been won, mescal wine or tequila began to be shipped beyond its national borders, and by the last quarter of the century, one-third of the tequila produced was being exported. Of this, 80 percent was sold to the United States, 12 percent to South America, and 8 percent to the United Kingdom.

By the beginning of the twentieth century (when the botanist Weber

Above: *One of the first bottles of Tequila Sauza.*

Facing page:
Millions of liters of tequila are exported in bulk for later bottling under brands and labels unknown in Mexico.

added his name to Jalisco's blue agave), tequila exports had fallen to 10 percent of total production and did not rise above 20 percent for many years, even during World War II. In 1974, however, due to important changes in agricultural practices that gave large tracts of land to peasant farmers, more agave was planted. This, along with an increase in the number of distilleries, created growth, and the involvement of transnational firms began to have an effect on the industry, since these firms bought large distilleries and opened new markets. In 1985 the exportation of tequila reached 31.1 million liters, and by 1998, 87 million liters.

Who imports tequila? • Today the principal customer is the United States, receiving more than 80 percent of tequila's worldwide exports. The remainder is shipped to Europe (13.5 percent), Latin America (3.5 percent), and the rest of the world (3 percent), so that now tequila is sold in over seventy countries. This is due in great part to the work of large international distributors, primarily from the United States and the United Kingdom, who market tequila in its original packaging, in bulk, or even stamped with their own labels.

Among the principal distributors (here listed by the volume of tequilas they handle) are Barton Brands, Ltd.; Brown-Forman Beverage Co.; Grand Metropolitan and its subsidiary Carrillon Imports;[12] Domecq Imports Co.;[13] Heaven Hill Distilleries, Inc.; Jim Beam Brands, Co.; and Joseph E. Seagram and Sons, Inc. The complete list includes a total of sixty-six firms. Some of them handle only large volumes of one brand, while others may manage several labels.

In most cases the national producers give preference to export over the domestic market. This is not only due to the lure of the dollar but because it gives producers a greater profit margin. Export markets can sustain higher prices, while domestic tequila sales are subject to 60 percent tax on the factory price as well as a 15 percent value-added tax. Nevertheless, the tax man is taken care of when the export income enters the country.

Where is the most tequila drunk? • The total production of tequila (1998 figures) stands at 170 million liters. Just over a half of this (86.5 million) is

Don Leonardo Rodríguez, owner of the Hacienda Corralejo distillery, Guanajuato, learned the art of distillation in Spain producing an acorn liqueur.

earmarked for export, leaving the rest (83.5 million liters) for local Mexican consumption.

In the United States most tequila is consumed in the large cities of California—San Diego is considered a paradise for tequila drinkers. Florida, New York, and Illinois come next.

In Europe, tequila's greatest success is in Germany, Holland, Belgium, and France, and it is increasing in Spain, Italy, Russia, and the United Kingdom. In the case of the United Kingdom, there is a paradox: though the two largest producers of tequila are now controlled by British firms, England is not yet a major consumer. A few years ago, more tequila was

Left: *Bottling and labeling production line in Tequila Sauza.*

Overleaf: *The agave ovens in the Herradura installations, Amatitán.*

77

drunk in Edinburgh than in London, but the current state of play shows England leading the field in tequila drinkers.

Another curious example is Spain. Very little tequila is consumed in Spain, though this country practically invented the original recipe.

The boom • Worldwide tequila sales are still soaring. Annually, tequila is being exported to more and more countries, and consumption seems to be without limit. At the present rate of growth Mexico's tequila exports could well surpass 100 million liters within a year or two. In Mexico itself there are more than 500 brands, and there are bars (such as Antonio's in Mexico City) that offer more than 350 selections!

In the export world the total number of tequila brands is unknown. It is said that there are more than 5,000 different labels in the United States alone. New ones seem to be appearing almost daily in both the domestic and foreign market. One man who has searched the world for tequila bottles and labels claims to have more than 1,500 different brands in his private collection.

In Mexico, a .75-liter bottle of the best tequila can cost as much as 3,500 pesos, while outside the country the price can soar to $1,000.

How did the boom begin? • During the 1960s tequila companies established alliances and joint ventures with producers and distributors abroad, often as part of commercial strategy but in some cases just in order to survive. Although it was widely sold and appreciated, it wasn't until the start of the 1990s that tequila began to flood the market. For example, in 1992, while he was beverage manager of the Ritz Carlton Hotel in Cancun, Ricardo Cisneros Beltrán, now an expert *tequilier*, had a bright idea that almost cost him his job:

I knew very little about tequila, but I saw that it was very popular with tourists, especially those from abroad. It occurred to me that it might be fun to create a section of the lobby bar devoted solely to tequila—a kind of "tequila corner." My boss thought I was crazy. How could I think of promoting tequila in a five-star hotel that served Louis XIII cognac? However, I organized everything subtly so that my idea would work. I created "happy hours" for tequila tasting and invited everyone to drink it in a new way . . . sipping and savoring. Customers had been used to drinking it fast, like a shot—Wham! Bam! This was how tequila had always been drunk. But "tasting" was something else. It was a hit!

We bought and served many of the classic tequila brands. They seemed quite similar at first, but I began to realize that there were definite, subtle differences among them, and my clients preferred the brands that contained 100 percent agave.

All of a sudden, at the beginning of 1993, a new tequila arrived, a fine reposado. The bottle was amber-colored and made from blown glass. It was a work of art. The price was also different, a lot more expensive than anything I'd seen. This tequila went like a rocket, and for me it marked the beginning of the boom, because from then on we began to get many new tequilas. Some were completely new labels, and others were just bottled differently. The tendency toward 100 percent agave in the blancos, reposados, and the añejos increased dramatically . . . and so did the customers. By this time my boss didn't think I was so crazy after all.

Let the good times roll! • All of the established tequila producers entered the race in the 1990s, making an extra effort to elevate (or sustain) both quality and presentation. Investors reopened distilleries that had been closed or built new ones. The fact that a family was descended from a long tradition of tequila makers did not necessarily mean that they knew how to make good tequila. Fortunately, there still remained "wise men" who had worked in the industry since childhood. They had seen their fathers and grandfathers make tequila, and knew the secrets.

Today, with the boom still reverberating around the world, tequila is not only a commercial success story but also has a certain cachet. Never in the fondly remembered past had tequila been able to walk arm and arm with cognac down Mexico City's fashionable Bucareli Street. Now it proudly rubs shoulders with the finest spirits in five-star hotels the world over.

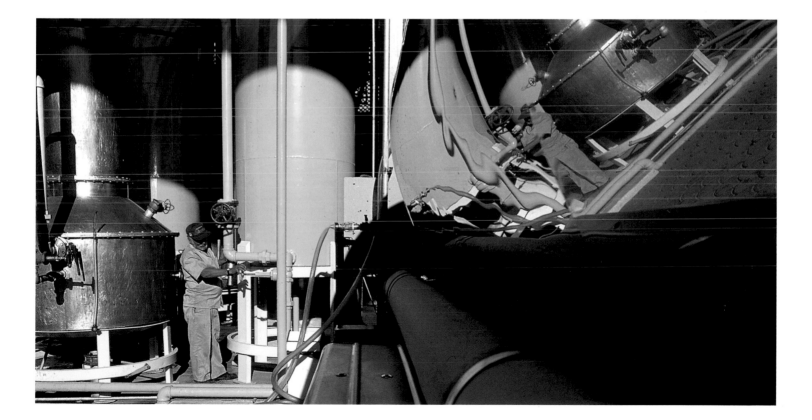

Hallelujah!

Above: *Filling a stainless steel tank with Orendain tequila for export.*

Facing page:
The filling of a settling barrel, Hacienda Corralejo, Guanajuato.

The lands and distilleries of Jalisco • In Jalisco one can visit many of the fifty to sixty tequila distilleries scattered throughout the state's fifteen municipalities, which account for almost all of the world's production. Our "tequila team"—photographer, writer, and tequila expert—spent the better part of two months traveling, learning, and tasting, tasting, tasting. . . .

Amatitán

Tequila Herradura, NOM 1119 • Of the four distilleries we visited in this area, we've chosen to describe Tequila Herradura. The board of directors of this company allowed us to explore their factory freely and to take photographs of the Hacienda de San José del Refugio, the two industrial plants, the warehouses, the big house, and just about every corner of their premises. The only places we were not allowed to enter were sealed warehouses that are, not surprisingly, deemed off-limits by the Council for the Regulation of Tequila, as well as the parts of the house the family still lives in.

Upon entering this ancient hacienda, one is transported back in time, to the beginning of the century. At the entrance are the workers' houses. Many of these people were born in them and have lived their whole lives here.

This is no rustic farm factory; San José del Refugio is a prosperous, beautifully run estate. New buildings blend with old ones that have been restored, and fields, barns, workers' cottages, and factory have been integrated to form a perfect whole.

The inhabitants of Amatitán believe that the tequilas from La Herradura are the best. They are produced on a great scale, though in a traditional way, and can pass any test of quality. Only a few years ago about 10,000 liters a day were produced, but a new distillery has been built on the premises, and today's daily production is between 30,000 and 35,000 liters.

Above: The Virgin of Guadalupe, symbol of faith in Mexico.

Opposite: "Golden Rain" tree framing the old Hacienda de San José del Refugio.

San José del Refugio, old distillery • At La Herradura the original distillery of San José del Refugio can still be visited. It is well worth the trip to see what tequila production must have been like at the beginning of the twentieth century. The distillery is so well preserved that a movie was made here to show how people lived in the past. What hard times they must have been! The place is dark, gloomy, and humid. Today there are dull yellow lamps where once there were candles and torches. One can see the great mill made of volcanic stone and the first fermentation vat, a great black hole

in the ground. This first vat is only a dozen steps away from the mill, but the last vat is more than sixty steps away, a long journey carrying full earthen jars weighing 130 or 180 pounds (60 or 80 kg) on one's head! Even farther away from the fermentation vats stand the old retorts. At a distance one can see two old storage vats made from white Mexican oak, a tree that is now extinct.

A sampling • On the top floor of the building, where the bottling takes place, is a lookout point from which one can gaze over the valley of Amatitán to the Tequila volcano in the distance. It is a lovely place to relax and taste the distillery's special tequila. Herradura makes one of the strongest white tequilas in Mexico (46 degrees GL), with an intense agave flavor and herbal aftertaste. If you let it lie on your tongue, the first sensation is almost too strong, but the aftertaste is soft and seductive. We also tasted the "silver," which is smoother (40 degrees GL).

Herradura's *reposados* have character, leaving a soft flavor with a slight taste of wood. The *añejo*, which has been aged for two and a half years, has an alluring wood taste that first appears dry but magically becomes sweet.

Left: *The distillation hall in the Herradura tequila factory. While many tequileros swear that good tequila requires copper stills, in Herradura stainless steel ones are used without sacrificing quality. Consumer demand remains high for all their brands.*

Opposite: *Automated bottling system in the Herradura tequila plant.*

Tequila

Tequila Orendain's La Mexicana, NOM 1110 ·
The gentleman in charge of La Mexicana greeted us warmly and then put us in the hands of Señor Pedro Juárez, a technician who works at the factory. He began by showing us the blue agaves in the front garden. Then he took us to the ancient but well-restored mill.

La Mexicana is truly a modern factory, with high-pressure cauldrons, industrial walkways, workers in uniform, and full safety equipment. The tequila emerging from the rectifying retorts was a mixed white (51/49). We tasted it and were well rewarded. On this particular visit we did not have a chance to try their Orendain Ollitas, which contains 100 percent agave, but several days later we lucked out. At La Mexicana the tequila is not bottled on-site but is sent in containers to the Orendain bottling plant or to its distributors in Florida.

Tequila Cuervo, NOM 1104[14] • How does one begin to describe one of Mexico's oldest tequila companies and the one that, incidentally, produces the most tequila? With La Rojeña, of course! This great distillery stands on the corner of Ramón Corona and José Cuervo Streets in Tequila, Jalisco. This plant alone produces 70,000 liters of tequila a day, and in addition the company has another distillery in Zapotlanejo.[15] Together, the plants produce as much as 210,000 liters a day.

The factory is well organized. Cuervo has also conserved, as far as possible, the traditional processes, combining them successfully with modern technology. The agave is cooked slowly in masonry ovens. The grinding is done in old mills sufficiently modernized to maximize efficiency. Fermentation vats made of stainless steel are placed in such an aesthetic way that they look like waterfalls. These are special vats with temperature gauges, something not found at most other tequila plants. Sophisticated safety controls are also installed throughout.

Cuervo's stellar product, in terms of sales, is the tequila *joven*, or "gold." This is an old product that the company used to launch itself into the United States. "Gold" is a mixed tequila (51 percent agave and 49 percent other sugars), aged for only the length of time it takes to give color, soften the flavor, and enrich it with an essence of wood. It is so popular in the United States that people generally ask for "Cuervo" instead of tequila.

Cuervo also makes several tequilas that contain 100 percent agave. In the area of *reposados* and the *blanco*, or "silver," it has launched several fine

Opposite: *Orendain, manufacturer of the traditional Ollitas tequila.*

Below: *José Cuervo Street, where tequila manufacturing began in earnest.*

products. Things get serious, though, when we bring up the subject of the *añejos*.

We thought that our visit was almost over when we were surprised and delighted by our hostess, who informed us that Señor Luis Yerenas Ruvalcaba, the regional director, had invited us to taste a new *añejo*.

As if this weren't enough, we were told that the tasting would take place in the Beckman family cellar, where, we suspected, Tequila Cuervo's finest treasures were stored. In the cellar we were greeted by the director as well as the engineers who supervise the plant's quality controls and production.

In the aging warehouses we had already seen hundreds of barrels of tequila that we supposed would be bottled and sold in celebration of the millennium. When they explained to us that they were tasting two last options for a new *añejo*, we wondered if this could possibly be?—did we dare hope?—was this the "tequila of the millennium?"

They explained to us that only a very select group of people was responsible for the tequila's production and quality control and that this team worked like a fraternity, meeting frequently to taste the various products, exchange ideas, and discuss the ideal conditions for creating their finest tequila. Among these tasters there are no hierarchies or leaders; only palates count. They have a great time and boast that they even have "homework:" everyone gets to take the tequila home, share it around, and collect opinions.

The tasting • Two brandy snifters stand before us. One is marked with a dark dot and the other is not. The tequila bottles are marked in the same way. These are two *añejo* tequilas. Glasses of water and salty crackers are available for cleaning the palate.

We sip from the glass that has no mark. On first impression it is soft, with "character"—a term used when alcohol vapors actually release a scent into one's nose. It is also slightly sweet with a wood flavor and a taste of mescal. We try it again, saturating our palate. Very inviting.

A sip of water, but no cracker • Next we proceed with the second, marked glass. Not as smooth, less character. There's a more spicy taste because the wood flavor is stronger. The mescal's there but harder to find. Once swallowed, it leaves a sweet taste and a craving for more.

Another drink of water. Yes, now we do want a cracker, and then more water. The tequila in the snifter without a mark is softer, has a richer mescal flavor, and it nearly gets our vote. But as the tasting progresses, the drink with the dot grows better and better and finally wins us over.

According to our own traveling tequila expert, both samples were extremely good. He explained that the unmarked glass still had the distant taste of herbs, nicely mixed with mescal, and that it had a strong character with a balanced taste of wood. The other *añejo* was superior, though, because it had a well-defined taste without losing the deep flavor of mescal, as well as an inviting quality.

Unfortunately, we were never allowed to know if our favorite was going to be Cuervo's tequila of the millennium, but we hope and believe that it will.

Tequila Sauza, NOM 1102 · The distillery located at 80 Francisco Javier Sauza Mora Street in Tequila, Jalisco, is very large, the largest after Cuervo. While we were doing our research there, local media reported that the distillery was planning an expansion that would, in the near future, put it in first place. In this distillery the process of hydrolization of the sugars includes two crude washes, one acid and the other enzymatic, before the shredded mescal is introduced.

As far as we know, the first 100 percent agave tequila that this firm produced was

their famous Hornitos, a *reposado*. In Don Javier Sauza's lifetime another *añejo* tequila called Tres Generaciones was introduced. Since we could not sample them in the factory, we decided to buy some Sauza tequilas to see how they compared.

The white (also known as silver) and the gold both make good margaritas. They are adequate mixed tequilas for cocktails and good enough to drink straight or with a sangrita chaser, or with the classic lime and salt. One does not always have to act the connoisseur.

The *reposado* is very good. It has a light honey color, good character, and a well-balanced mescal taste. The first sip is smooth, but it leaves behind a slightly cloying taste that is a bit confusing to the palate, and lacks the charm of their white.

Sauza's *añejos* cannot compete with the several others that vie with them for first place. They lack character even though they have a pleasant, smooth flavor. Ten years ago they were better, despite being made of a mixture of musts.

That said, in the United States and in the United Kingdom Sauza products are very successful, and bartenders claim that their 100 percent agave *reposado* is the best for making a good margarita.

La Tequileña, NOM 1146 • The story behind this distillery is very interesting. It was founded in the 1960s by one of the Orendain brothers,[16] and at the beginning of the 1980s it was bought by Bacardi, which modernized and expanded the plant so that it now has the capacity to produce more than 9,000 liters of tequila a day. This brand of mixed tequila was called Xalisco, and it still exists today.

In 1987 La Tequileña was sold again to a company that made brandy. They could not make a success of it, and in 1990 it was sold to Don Enrique Fonseca, one of the largest producers of agave in the state of Jalisco. In the hands of this businessman the company thrived,

and by 1992 it was producing high-quality tequilas made of 100 percent agave. This well-equipped company has a reputation for excellent quality control and consequently has played an important role in the new tequila boom. Investors who want to produce their own brand of tequila often go to La Tequileña for this service.[17]

Above: *The installation of a triple-distillation tower heralds a new era in the manufacturing process at La Tequileña.*

Opposite: *The main entrance to La Perseverancia, the Tequila Sauza factory.*

Another tasting to tempt us • Our tequila expert gave us a pleasant surprise at La Tequileña when we were asked to try three samples of *añejo* tequila, aged for three years, which were in the final running and had been produced for the Suave Patria company. On this particular occasion, everything was far simpler. There were no tablecloths or brandy snifters. The tequila samples were in Erlenmeyer flasks and liqueur glasses. The first sample was discarded immediately because of its incorrect proportions. The mescal and wood had not married. Far from feeling embarrassed, the technician smiled: this was a trap, perhaps to test our tequila expert, but no one was fooled.

The other two samples were quite good. One was very smooth and sweet, but the taste of mescal crowded out the taste of wood. It seemed closer to a *reposado* that had been aged for eight months than a true *añejo*. The second was also smooth, but with character, and it possessed a strong wood flavor that was spicy at first and then grew slightly sweet. It was delicious. To novices like us they both seemed good, but our expert thought that the second sample was the better, though it still needed a little adjustment to deepen the mescal flavor.

Atotonilco

7 Leguas, NOM 1120 • At the beginning of the twentieth century, Don José González founded several distilleries in Atotonilco. They were not the first, but due to the chaotic conditions of the Mexican Revolution they were the only ones that lasted. At his death they were passed on to his nephew Ignacio González Vargas, who bought the distillery next to the river,[18] and Julio González, Ignacio's first cousin, who as a young man began to run his business independently.

Ignacio González's distillery was called El Centenario, as it was established in 1910—the centennial of Mexico's independence. Besides its mixed variety, El Centenario produced 100 percent agave tequila that the people of Atotonilco were very proud of:

"The people from Tequila have only beaten us with their name," says "7" González, proudly.[19] "All tequila is good, but Atotonilco's is the best. And, of all those produced in Atotonilco, I believe that mine is beyond compare. We are not the largest firm and I do not want to say that the tequila produced by the other González's is far behind, but if we are talking taste, mine is superior."

Although the city of Tequila gave
its name to the drink, other regions
in Jalisco now have vast tracts of
land dedicated to the cultivation
of the blue agave.
One such area is the colonial
town of Atotonilco in the eastern
part of the state.

93

When Don Ignacio died, his children operated El Centenario successfully. When the boom came, they expanded and built a new industrial plant called La Triunfadora. These plants use both copper and steel stills, and the contents of each are mixed together. The portions used in the mix are kept secret, since they define the characteristics of their *blancos*, *reposados*, and the exclusive *añejos*.

The aging takes place in warehouses that are not large but filled to the roof with barrels. Because of this confined space, the smell of aging tequila is extraordinary. A dedicated connoisseur would enjoy living here!

7 Leguas, the horse of long ago • Our host invited us to taste one of his *añejo* tequilas called El Patrón, which is apparently made only for export. In actual fact this same tequila is sold in Mexico under the name 7 Leguas Black Label, but even the manufacturer has trouble finding it.

The first sip of this tequila had charm and character.

Above: *Don Fernando González, master tequilero and one of the owners of 7 Leguas.*

Opposite: *The production process at La Triunfadora, one of the 7 Leguas plants.*

The taste of mescal came and went, overtaken by the flavor of wood. The barrel that it had been aged in was very mature, so it neither pricked our tongues nor left us asking for more. It had an aroma that was very light, almost like corn sugar, and it seemed to have body, but even that disappeared after a while, giving way to a sweet aftertaste of mescal.

Sometime later we tried the white 7 Leguas, in the Campestre restaurant on the outskirts of Atotonilco. The arguments began. Those of us who are passionate about white tequila thought it was wonderful. Others demurred. So we would not come to blows, we agreed not to compare it to that paramount white, the proverbial Herradura, although in our hearts we knew that the 7 Leguas whites could hold their own

even there. They weren't exactly "brothers," but they could be "good friends." This tequila from Atotonilco was less charming than the one from Amatitán, but in taste, nothing compares.

The drinks specialist Bob Emmons says that 7 Leguas tequilas are among the best. Currently, they are bestsellers among the so-called super-premium brands. These tequilas are considered some of the most glamorous and rewarding, and if you're planning a tasting, they should certainly be included.[20]

"7 Leguas was the name of the horse that Villa most esteemed. When trains whistled, the horse halted and reared. 7 Leguas was the horse that Villa most esteemed."

"What's in the pot comes out in the spoon"

Tres Magueyes, NOM 1118 • Don Julio González, from Atotonilco, Jalisco, founded his first distillery in the 1930s, when he was only seventeen years old. He had already acquired much valuable experience from his family. As a boy he had worked with his uncle and learned the ancient method of making mescal wine in underground ovens, the way they did before steam cauldrons were invented.

Don Julio's second company was called Tres Magueyes, a name chosen after much brainstorming among friends and family. The distillery itself was called La Primavera.[21]

Though Don Julio's lands are scattered around, they add up to 800 hectares, some belonging to him and some rented. He showed us a few of his fields and explained to us the planting, replanting, spacing, and fertilization techniques. He also demonstrated how to distinguish land that was good for planting agave, and pointed out how to identify ground that had been flooded by rains and become infertile. Don Julio explained, "The plant is where it all starts. If the mescal is good, the tequila will be good. What's in the pot will come out in the spoon. We have cared about this. People notice, and this is why our tequila is succeeding so well."

We made a stop at the country estate of Francisco González, the son of Don Julio and currently president of Tres Magueyes and vice president of the Council for the Regulation of Tequila. Here we were invited to taste the family's special tequilas. These are stored in a row of barrels under a bar in a room opening onto an attractively decorated living and dining room. The beautiful murals on the walls took our breath away.

We were given an *añejo* called Don Julio Real (one of the most expensive and prestigious of all tequilas), as well as a sample of their *reposado* and *blanco*. The latter wasn't really white, but seemed more like a *reposado*. They were all excellent.

Arandas and Jesús María

In these two municipalities of Los Altos there are almost a dozen distilleries, and the tequilas from Arandas in particular enjoy considerable prestige not only in Jalisco but throughout Mexico and abroad.

Tequila Tapatío, NOM 1139 • La Alteña was the original name given to the Camarena family's distillery. Over time it came to belong to Felipe Camarena Hernández, whom everyone in Arandas knew simply as Don Felipe. This gentleman deeded his company to his son, Felipe Camarena Orozco, a chemical engineer who is known in this city as "Engineer Camarena."

Today, Señor Camarena is over seventy years old and has stayed on as adviser to his children, Carlos and Felipe Camarena Curiel, both highly trained professionals who manage the firm, with their sisters' help.

Tequila Tapatío is rooted in Arandas, and although it is a relatively small producer, this is the preferred tequila of many experts. Tesoro (Treasure) de Don Felipe Blanco has been very successful, to the extent that it is considered one of the three top white tequilas available in Mexico and has been given a four-star rating, a rare distinction among white tequilas.[22]

At the distillery we tasted the white tequila. The two Camarena brothers advised us that tradition dictates guests must try the tequila out of a bull's horn.

"Here we have two horns," Carlos Camarena told us as we approached the wooden barrel containing white tequila. "This one is the classic horn for tasting tequila."

"Or would you prefer," added his brother, "a goat's horn, for those who want to break with tradition?" (A goat's horn—cuerno de chivo—is the popular name for a type of automatic rifle.)

We meekly went for the bull, and all of us passed the horn test. Afterward, we had a chance to watch el batidor, the human beater, in action. It's easy to imagine what other activities the naked man in the vat might be up to! Fortunately, tequila goes through a distillation process, and the high temperatures will sterilize anything.

Ahhh! *Very good! Tapatío is as sweet as a tequila should be. It has a lot of character but is smooth both in taste and aroma, good at the beginning, but better at the end. Different. Yes, very different from other tequilas found in Jalisco and Los Altos. The taste of mescal is intense, and elegance is sacrificed for charm. It is so good, one might easily drink too much.*

Corralejo

Tequila Corralejo, NOM 1368 • In the state of Guanajuato, in the municipality of Pénjamo, we find Hacienda Corralejo. This distillery is a combination of cultural history and tradition, unusual because it is one of the only NOM distilleries producing good tequila outside the state of Jalisco. This lovely ex-hacienda is renowned as the birthplace of Miguel Hidalgo, father of Mexican independence. Immediately one sees the old copper stills, which the proprietor, Don Leonardo Rodríguez, tells us started out life distilling acorns in Spain. Encouraged by his success there, he returned to Mexico and applied the same processes to the distillation of agave. At the front entrance traditional masonry ovens and agave mills give out an inviting odor. Inside the hacienda several rooms are set up as a museum dedicated to the history of Mexican independence.

Drinking tequila:
techniques, tricks, and tall tales

Tequila is legendary, surrounded by a wealth of myths, rites, and conventions. We shall explore these from the standpoint of the experts as well as those who only care about the pleasure they get from drinking. Tequila is everything: an aperitif, a gastronomic treat, and a good digestive. After a hard day it relaxes the soul. At a party it fills the heart with euphoria.

And, for those who drink beyond the limit, it can raise the dead and become a passport to purgatory. Drinking is delightful. Hangovers are humiliating!

Drinking tequila by the traditional technique of knocking it back in one gulp has been the norm. As an old barfly in a cantina in Tequila explained when he saw us trading shots of El Tequileño, a favorite of the establishment,

"That is the way one of my best friends drank white. He drank it like water.

I dilute mine with ice or a soft drink. If I don't, what happened to my friend will

happen to me. He ended up chasing his goats all over the mountains . . .

even though he never even had any goats!"

Some experts say that one should taste tequila with the tip of the tongue. Apparently, this area is the most resistant. If you let the liquid go directly to the back of the tongue, which is sensitive to bitter tastes, you are forced to swallow fast because the taste is so strong it takes your breath away.

Amateurs compare drinking tequila to lighting a fire in one's mouth and then instinctively wanting it to be quickly extinguished! This impulse is resolved in a variety of ways.

Lime and salt • Mexican green lemons come in two varieties: bitter lemons, which are cultivated in Michoacán, Colima, and the states surrounding Jalisco, and the large, less acidic seedless lemons, which are grown on a large scale in Nuevo León. In English, both these lemons are known as limes, and they both serve well as tequila fire extinguishers.

A traditional tequila drinker who marries his tequila with sips of lime and salt usually follows this sequence:

The limes are cut in quarters next to a plate of sea salt. Single or double shot glasses are at the ready, the latter being especially used for white tequila. The order is simple. First, a small sip is taken in order to savor the tequila and get acquainted with the drink. This first sip is not "extinguished," since it is quickly followed by a long drink that slides over the tongue on its way to one's inner soul. An instant later, one bites the lime in order to soothe the tongue, and a bit of salt placed on the back of one's hand is then licked up smartly. To skip this step, place the salt directly on the lime.

Above: Ricardo Cisneros, tequilier, tasting a genuine Don Felipe treasure in the traditional horn of a bull.

Opposite: Lime and salt, the seasoned partners of tequila.

Page 100: Pedro Armendáriz in the 1947 film Juan Charrasqueado. Pascual Espinoza Collection.

"If you're drinking to forget

first pay your debt"

This custom of extinguishing tequila by using lime and salt has been a tradition for many years. However, over time new methods have developed. Some drinkers squeeze a lime beforehand, then mix it with the tequila in the shot glass. This can be disappointing, since contact with air makes the lime bitter.

Some say the whole process should require the use of only one hand. This is done by alternately picking up the glass of tequila and the lime between one's thumb and index finger, while the salt lies in a small mound on the back of the same hand. It takes a fair amount of practice to get this right so that the salt does not scatter down your shirtfront or end up all over your mustache.

Sara García and Pedro Infante in the 1948 film Dicen que soy mujeriego. *Pascual Espinoza Collection.*

Other fire extinguishers · *Sangrita* · An old recipe for extinguishing the fire varies in different areas of Mexico. Over time and with the influence of tourists it has gone through many changes. The people of Jalisco are offended when one suggests that *sangrita* may not have been invented there, although evidence indicates that this unusual drink most likely came from the Yucatan or Campeche, where most bitter oranges grow. The *sangrita* from Yucatan is prepared with the juice of these oranges, salt, and a mixture of chiles, which sometimes includes the famous *habanero* chile. They do not use lime, and frankly, it is unnecessary.

Sangrita

(Recipe provided by the Martínez Gallardo family, Guadalajara)

2 ancho chiles
(approx. 1 oz. [25 g] each),
lightly roasted, cleaned, and
soaked
1 tablespoon finely chopped onion
(approx. 3.5 oz. [100 g])
2 cups orange juice
1 tablespoon grenadine
juice of 1 lime

Place all ingredients in the blender and puree.

In the west of Mexico (Michoacán, Jalisco, Colima, and Nayarit), *sangrita* recipes, originally based on a mixture of orange juice, salt, red chile, and pomegranate syrup, have suffered notable changes. Here, someone decided to add tomato juice, probably to please a foreign palate, and this strange new combination became very popular. So, you "catch fire" with tequila and "extinguish" with *sangrita*. Macho drinkers consider this something only ladies do, but actually it's a general practice, especially for those drinking white.

The bricklayer's drinking spree • Extinguishing the tequila blaze with beer is a traditional Mexican practice, and as both drinks have long been associated with the lower classes, someone decided to call this custom "the bricklayer's drinking spree." In truth, it is now done at every social level.

It can be approached in two ways. First you take a drink of tequila; then, in order to extinguish it, you down a beer, usually a lager. Another more daring procedure is called the

submarine, and this consists of carefully placing the shotglass full of tequila in an empty, inverted beer glass, then righting it and filling it with beer so that the two drinks mingle each time the drinker takes a sip.

The end result of drinking beer and tequila is that you get drunk quickly, which is why they say bricklayers do it. "It's a cheap high," they say.

Changuirongos. During the 1940s, in the city of Guadalajara, a soft drink called Royal Crown Cola from the United States became fashionable. Someone got the bright idea of extinguishing tequila quickly, but without giving up the lime. Tequila, lime juice, and cola were mixed together. This is how the first recipe for a *changuirongo* appeared. Later, it was decided that you could also add salt, and instead of rimming the glass with it, you could

add it directly to the liquid. This kind of *changuirongo* was called a "Rusa" (Russian).

Consumed in this way, the mixture just slips down your throat delightfully, but there's a catch: in order to taste the tequila through the strong cola, lime, and salt flavors, you are forced to pour a large amount of tequila. The result is that after a few *changuirongos* you could end up standing before the Zapopan Virgin, begging to live a little longer.

Another version of the *changuirongo* is now currently in fashion in Guadalajara. The tequila is diluted with ice and a fizzy grapefruit drink. Lime and salt are optional.

Mexican fiesta in Cancun: extravagant sombreros, juggling waiters, and patrons who can't wait to run the tequila gauntlet.

Muppets are another, more famous version. Here, small shots are prepared with equal measures of tequila and a cold lemon or grapefruit soft drink like Sprite. The ingredients are mixed and shaken and then banged against a table so that the gas from the soft drink turns into foam, which is then knocked back in one gulp. In the United States these drinks are called "slammers."

Cucarachas, or "cockroaches," are suicidal. This is a drink made with tequila, a coffee liqueur such as Kahlua, and Cointreau, mixed in a glass. A short straw is inserted into the drink, which is then ignited. The *cucaracha* drinker has to suck up the liquid before the flames destroy the straw . . . and then commend his (or her) soul to God!

"Muppets:" a real time bomb, made with tequila and a lemon or grapefruit soda.

Bubbles and myths • For the modern drinker wanting to try tequila, to satisfy the senses without losing them, the options for honoring the palate couldn't be greater.

When tequila is poured into a clear glass such as a brandy snifter, bubbles form. Sometimes there is just one big bubble, and sometimes many small ones appear, quickly moving toward the surface, where they stick to the side of the glass, looking like a string of pearls. When only one bubble appears, it forms very quickly and then slowly disappears. The presence of these bubbles has a direct relationship to the tequila's alcoholic content and body. If they do not form or if they disappear quickly, it means that the strength of the tequila is poor, or *cortado* (cut). When bubbles form and then remain and break at the edge of the glass, creating a lovely necklace just above the liquid, you know that you are in the presence of a work of art!

Above: The string of pearls is a good indicator of the body and alcoholic content of a quality tequila.

Opposite: During the past fifteen years, the image of tequila has changed. It is no longer considered just a quick route to a hangover but rather a refined and fresh-tasting beverage, which in the case of good añejos like 7 Leguas' D'Antaño Reserva is served in a cognac glass like any quality after-dinner drink.

After a feast • After a good, filling meal a strong drink goes down nicely and helps the digestion. This is the moment for *añejo* tequilas. One, two, or even three glasses of a good *añejo* tequila are a commendable conclusion to any meal, though after three glasses of *añejo* anything can happen. If a person likes to smoke, he or she can drink the tequila accompanied by a good cigar from Veracruz or Havana. In Mexico, this ritual is called a *desempance*, which literally means "to take away your full stomach."

Tequila lore offers many solutions to life's problems and dilemmas: if you are sad, a glass of tequila will "pick you up," or in the worst case, make you weep even more. If you are happy, it will make you happier. If you are irritable, tequila will soothe your nerves. If your girlfriend leaves you,

> **"Drink well, eat well ... and wait for the end to come."**

it will inspire you to look for another. If you are suffering, it will make you sing. But you should never drink tequila when you are angry, because that will only make it worse. Tequila is said to be a brawler's drink because too much can make one violent.

The hangover fantasy • Tequila's dark legends, and there are many, come and go with fashion, and they are fed by people talking about their own experiences while under the influence.

Ten years ago, people in Mexico who dared to say that tequila did not produce a hangover were thought to be naive. Then the boom came, and there were wild rumors claiming that well-distilled, 100 percent agave tequila did not give you a hangover! Suddenly, it seemed to become an aperitif, a digestive, a sexual catalyst, so pure and natural that it might be injected straight into your veins instead of serum. Magic!

One thing is true (and this we can swear to before the Virgin of Guadalupe): if someone claims to feel fine the morning after drinking a liter of tequila, though it may have cost a thousand dollars, that person has sold his soul to the devil.

Labels • In the past, labels on tequila bottles contained graphics that were only concerned with marketing and promotion. Sometimes these were very beautiful and well designed but there was never any mention of the tequila's properties.

In the 1940s and 1950s, the tequila industry formalized labeling practices; labels changed, since the authorities demanded that each bottle display the manufacturing permits along with details of alcoholic content and other official information. However, the organization of tequila manufacturers took nearly twenty years to agree on a standard that would satisfy everyone.

The latest criteria for bottle labeling date from 1994, and require that the label[23] must be clear, legible, and contain all the information in Spanish.[24] It must include:

1. Name of the product and the official identification (NOM) of the distillery.

2. The kind of tequila (*blanco, joven, reposado, añejo,* or mixed with coffee, syrups, etc.)

3. Net content in liters or milliliters.[25]

4. Alcoholic content expressed in degrees GL or percentage of alcohol by volume at 68°F (20°C).

5. The distillery's name or trade name, address, and registration number in the taxpayer's list.

6. Registered trademark.

7. Location of manufacture and the inscription *Hecho en México* ("Made in Mexico").

8. The words "Abuse of this product is dangerous to your health."

The information in numbers 1, 6, and 7 must appear on the face of the label, while the others can be placed anywhere on the bottle.

The Council for the Regulation of Tequila also has its own requirements. If the tequila is certified as 100 percent agave, the label must state "CRT 100 percent agave" and display the seal that attests to the tequila's place of origin. The remaining space on the labels is free to be printed with the company's own logos and slogans.

Bottles and bottle tops • Here we enter a world in which laws and reality do not necessarily coincide. This is due to the great number of exceptions that occur during the exporting of tequila.

Originally, tequila was not even bottled. The practice was to place it in small wooden barrels, with or without a spigot, which people bought and carried home. They also used clay jugs or gourds as containers.[26] Though glass bottles had been used since the end of the nineteenth century, industrial use on a grand scale began only in the 1920s and 1930s.

"Drinking, drinking, drinking,

until we drop!

Long live Noé

the great patriarch!

Why, why, why?

Because he invented

the delicious spirit

mescal, mescal,

mescal."

The classic tequila bottle, called *pachita* or *pachoncita*, is the small bottle one sees in the Mexican movies of this period, one that slips easily inside a pocket, and memorialized in the line, "Hey, pass the penicillin."[27]

Currently the law states that a bottle, whatever its size or shape, has to have an additional seal, since there are devious people who either copy the bottles or refill them. Some companies, especially those that export, have begun to put a seal or label on the bottle caps as well. Choosing a tequila by looking at the bottle is not easy. Brands and their different presentations increase on a daily basis. Only a few years ago, if one went to the liquor store to buy tequila it was easy to choose among a Cuervo, Sauza, Orendain, Herradura, Eucario González, Xalisco, Viuda de Romero, and a few others. In bars or restaurants you could find four or five options, maybe ten in some of the larger cantinas. Things have changed. Today, in any small liquor store, one can find at least fifteen different brands, and larger stores may display up to forty.

Over the past years, tequila has acquired fame not only as a quality drink but also for the breathtaking variety in the design of its bottles and labels. The bottles appearing on pages 112-120 are courtesy of Don Juan Francisco Torres Landa, whose collection includes more than 1,500 different tequilas.

However, the tequila boom is now evident all over the world, to the point that some bars and restaurants have become veritable tequila museums. These places sell hundreds of different brands, each in a distinct bottle with varying bottle tops and labels.

Some tequilas are bottled in handmade containers of blown glass or ceramics that look like jugs or fine liqueur bottles. Some are very tall and slim, and others short and squat. They may be square or even round. They come in dark and transparent glass, and the bottle tops can be made of plastic, cork, wood, or a combination of these three. Many bottles are made in such a way that they cannot be filled again, but some manufacturers don't bother with this, perhaps because they are confident of their product, or maybe because much of it is exported to countries that do not have laws controlling bottle tops.

The price • Blown glass or handmade ceramic bottles are truly works of art. Often the bottle is more valuable than the alcohol inside, and as they are sold together, the price can be fierce—as much as 500 to 1,000 pesos in Mexico (about $50–$100). At a bar, one serving of these tequilas can cost between 100 and 500 pesos, while a glass of excellent white tequila, bottled in a conventional way and found in a bar 600 miles away, can cost a mere 25 pesos.

"water is to be employed, tequila to be enjoyed"

If the tequila inside the bottle is very special, a high price tag might be justified, but beware: one has to decide if one is buying the tequila or buying a beautiful bottle in a beautiful box.

When buying fine *añejos*, one has to make the same decisions one would make selecting a fine cognac. Cuervo Reserva de la Familia and Herradura Selección Suprema (Supreme Selection) are among the most expensive. They are worth it, but one has to spend between 1,000 and 3,000 pesos for a .75-liter bottle.

And what about the cheapo bottles of tequila that cost 15 pesos per liter? The answer is simple: draw up your will before you drink!

Drinking tequila in Tequila • If one wants to drink tequila far from the tourist traps, in a small, authentic village atmosphere, one might go to a cantina called La Capilla in Tequila. The owner is Don Javier—"Javiercito" to his friends—who in his youth was a barrel maker, like his father and grandfather.

La Capilla is not a luxurious place. Quite the contrary, it is a modest cantina that has three doors but only four tables and eight bar stools designed for eight skinny customers. There are not many different kinds of tequila, maybe five brands, and the bar does not sell food or cigarettes. What La Capilla does have is Don Javier, who has soaked up the history of Tequila for over sixty years. La Capilla is also a hangout for Don Javier's friends, who are the life and soul of the village. Some are modest farmers, some wealthy agave planters. Here a day laborer can rub shoulders with his boss.

In this cantina, drunken pigheadedness and other kinds of outlandish behavior are outlawed. If a customer drinks too much, everyone joins in an amusing hoax: they all stand up, say good-bye, and leave through one of the doors. Don Javier proceeds to close his canteen, and the drunkard has no option but to leave. La Capilla is located on a corner so that the doors exit onto different streets. Don Javier makes sure that the drunken customer leaves through the front, while the customers who pretended to leave slide back in through the side door.

Opposite: *Don Javier prepares yet another* changuirongo *in La Capilla, a bar of renown in the city of Tequila.*

Overleaf: *Reproduction of a José Cuervo publicity poster.*

"Who in this life is not familiar
with the well-known betrayal
that follows a sad love affair?
Who does not then go to the cantina
demanding a tequila,
and demanding a song?"

Living tequila:
a drink turned national symbol

 Can one consider tequila a decisive cultural factor? Has rum had an influence on the development of Cuba? Is whiskey part of Scottish highland culture? Can you talk about the Russians without taking vodka into account?

Until the first part of the seventeenth century tequila did not exist as a word, and for several hundred years after the first blue tequila agaves began to be distilled, pulque remained the

typical drink of Mexico. However, if you were to ask foreigners what drink characterizes contemporary Mexico they would not hesitate to say tequila, as would ninety-nine out of a hundred Mexicans, even though in some parts, cane spirit is preferred.

People from the state of Jalisco tell colorful and touching stories about the meaning of tequila in their own lives. A son of the Mexican Revolution, Macedonio told us his:

I was born in 1920 in the countryside of Jalisco. There I was baptized, and until I was sixteen, I lived

in the town of Degollado. All of my family were peasants or day laborers. They worked with sugarcane

in Tepatitlán and harvested mescal in Amatitán, Tequila, El Arenal, and Venustiano Carranza. We

worked where we could and were very poor. I only began to eat with a knife and fork when I went to

military school in 1939. I'd seen eating utensils, but my "fork" was a piece of tortilla.

Every day we ate corn and squash. Sometimes we ate the yucca from the mescal plant cooked with chile,

cactus, horse, or donkey meat—only rarely beef or goat. We were Christians, very Catholic, but can you

understand what this was like? "Abuelita," my maternal grandmother, did not even know how to speak

Spanish. She was from Nayarit and spoke in a regional dialect. On my father's side everyone was pretty

light-skinned. I think that somewhere along the way a French soldier must have liked my great grandmother.

But I was born as dark as the earth and proud of it. Most adults drank mescal that came from Tequila or

who knows where. My father and his two elder brothers liked it a lot, though they never missed a day's

work or behaved badly. We had a little house halfway up the hill. During the presidency of Plutarco Elías

Calles, my father was given a hectare of land on the side of the mountain, as were many others. The new

owners proceeded to fell trees and clear the land to plant mescal. Nobody knew a damn thing about the

scientific names of the plants, the only thing that mattered to them was that the lands should turn blue

with the color of mescal. The companies buying the mescal were always tough bargainers. Some were

from Cuervo, others belonged to Sauza, in Tequila. One small company belonged to the Hacienda de

San José del Refugio, in Amatitán. It was difficult to carry the mescal so far. I was talking about the

elders or adults. Well, let me tell you, in those days, when a kid was twelve he was already a man.

Today, you still get spanked at that age. In 1932, when I was twelve, my brother Artemio, the eldest,

put a poncho on my back and told me to follow him. My father and the rest of us left before dawn. We

walked for two hours until we got to some fields covered with thousands and thousands of mescals, where

we found other crews working. Some guy wearing an

expensive hat told us to get to work in the furrows. My

brother Artemio taught me how to harvest and do the

work I'd seen done all my life: cut the leaves from the

mescal plant, trim the root, and leave it round like a ball.

Nobody there called them pineapples. None of us had

ever seen a pineapple. Not even in our dreams! I am

talking about the sweet pineapples.

God, they're good!

As a writer, you might find this very romantic. It is lovely

to watch a harvester work, you think. How picturesque, you say. Then, when the tequila is finally made,

the rich people drink it and talk about life, love, the must, distilled spirits, and whatever other crap comes

to mind. But I saw other things. I've seen a harvester cut his foot off with the sharp coa simply because

he missed the mark or because he was tired or sick. I saw my father, my brothers, and my uncles give their

whole lives to these fields—planting, tending, harvesting, and then, worst of all, having to carry the great balls of mescal to the carts or trucks. I also carried them and know how your soul shrinks when they put a 150-pound ball of mescal on your head. When I was a boy I also saw how poor people got drunk on tequila. Poverty made them drink to forget. Over there, in Degollado, I saw so much blood in and outside the cantinas that it made me want to vomit. Peasants and ranchers, full of mescal, cut each other to pieces with their machetes, coas, and axes. They shot each other just because they were looking for a fight. You could see the blood fill their shirts as they were hit. And you can't imagine the violence that existed in Jalisco during the Cristero Rebellion.

I have to tell you how I managed to get an education. One day, on the recommendation of a friend of a man who was a friend of my father, I was able to get the forms, fill them out, and get into the military academy. There I became a different kind of man. When I came out, as a second lieutenant, I was lucky. I was assigned to a regiment in the south of Jalisco, my home. I was there for several years. There was peace then, but not much. You see, the troops there had always been tough on young, inexperienced lieutenants who had just arrived from military school. The sergeant never let us forget how green we were. I learned to ride, and in time I was lucky enough to pick up charro riding. I loved it but couldn't give it much time because I had other work. When I was still quite young I became a captain, and soon a major.

Then I asked for permission to study at the National University so that I might have a future. Although I was pretty old for it I went to high school and then studied to be an accountant. I did all this without leaving the army. I had to support my parents and other relatives who were in bad shape. I can tell you, and with pride, that I pulled it off.

Sometime around 1960 things started to go well. I began to earn money from my small accounting business and managed to help my people. The truth is I turned them away from our ancestral trade. You see, one of my main goals was to make sure that no kid in my family would have to harvest a single mescal ever again. I wanted them to study and prosper. It's worked—more or less. What hurts is that life did not give me enough time to help my dear mother, who died as she lived—poor.

I became a good charro rider. I bought a grand, colonial house in San Angel, in Mexico City and restored every corner of it. My sons and daughters became charros too, and they also live well, but I make sure they know who they are and don't forget where they came from. Now, let's talk about the pleasures of tequila and not the hardships of survival.

"For all bad things, mescal; for all good things as well"

"What is it with Jalisco that has made tequila so famous?"

A brief history • The ancient Nahua people passed through Jalisco in their transmigration through Mexico's central plateau. It is said that they came out of Nayarit, a region that is part of Jalisco today. Some historians say that the mythical Aztlán Chicomostoc is in Nayarit, while others think that it is on the edges of Lake Chapala. One group of these immigrants were called Aztecs, though they later changed their name to Mexicans when Mexi, the plant god, revealed himself and said to these peoples: "As of today, you shall no longer call yourselves Aztecs, you will be Mexicans."[28] If this is true, then the Mexican nation evolved, or at least got its name, in Jalisco.

During the conquest, the original inhabitants of Jalisco resisted the Spaniards for longer than did the Mexica. It took Hernán Cortés only a few years to vanquish the Mexica, while Nuño de Guzmán required more than twenty years to conquer the various ethnic groups living in Jalisco and southeastern Zacatecas.

During the struggle for independence, Father Hidalgo took refuge in Guadalajara, where he did two very significant and contradictory things: he allowed terrible and unjustified butchery to occur, and he heroically abolished slavery.[29]

Above: *The figure of Father Miguel Hidalgo in José Clemente Orozco's mural, Government Palace, Guadalajara, Jalisco.*

Above: Luis Aguilar and Jorge Negrete exchange songs and yawns in the 1952 film Tal para Cual.

During the French intervention, the lands of Jalisco were bathed in blood. This is no exaggeration. The people of Jalisco, warriors since pre-Hispanic times, did not give a moment's peace to their invaders or the traitors who supported them. It was the inhabitants of Tequila who succeeded in capturing the famous outlaw known as "El Tigre de Alica," who had joined Coronel Dupin on his bloody campaign of counter-insurgency against the Mexican guerrillas.

But the history of Jalisco was not always glorious. This is the state where Victoriano Huerta, the traitor who assassinated President Francisco Madero, was born. It was also here that a great part of the Cristero Rebellion of the 1920s took place. Jalisco, at times, has been known as a land of cutthroats.

Three ingredients: radio, cinema and television

• At the beginning of the twentieth century, Mexicans were only drinking about 600,000 liters of tequila a year, mostly in Guadalajara and Mexico City. The benefits of mass publicity had not yet reached the general public, but with the arrival of the movies and radio, things changed.

In the 1940s one segment of the national movie industry attempted to recapture many of Mexico's popular traditions. These movie directors and scriptwriters tried to ensure that the old traditions were filmed in an authentic way. But there were others who failed, filming cowboys from Guadalajara in Jalisco or muleteers from Sayula in Morelos! Some movies were shot in the beautiful towns of Jalisco, relating stories that really occurred in places that looked more like Querétaro. Many movies were made that could have taken place anywhere in Mexico, with a typical mixture of colonial buildings, small adobe houses, towns surrounded by maguey and cactus, ranchers with enormous straw hats, and riders with silver spurs.

The main reason for making these movies, however, was to give their star actors an excuse to sing. The songs came from all over the country and included *huapangos* from

JOHN WAYNE

9570 Wilshire Blvd., Suite 400
Beverly Hills, California 90212
October 13, 1977

Mr. Francisco Javier Sauza
Av. La Paz 2660
Guadalajara, Jalisco, Mexico

My dear friend:

It seems our varied activities have prevented our wished for "get together." My home telephone number is 714/646-9740. I have your 'phone numbers; and if they will ever give me a little rest, I shall call you.

Your very special product has become as necessary in our household as air and water.

As we keep saying, "Hasta la vista amigo."

Sincerely,

John Wayne

JW/ps

Top: Letter from the famous film star John Wayne to his friend Francisco Javier Sauza.

Tamaulipas, *corridos* from Nuevo León, or *sones* from Jalisco. They were composed for specific singers depending on their range and style and the scene being filmed. A song written for Jorge Negrete, an opera singer before he became a *charro* cowboy, was very different from one composed for Pedro Infante, a charismatic performer but one whose voice could not compare to Negrete's.

In this cinematic school, tequila became a famous image that was exported all over Mexico and the world. The rancher, *charro* cowboy, brawler, drunk, gambler, gunslinger, and Casanova on horseback always had a bottle of tequila to hand. There was, it has to be admitted, an element of truth in this.

The radio industry also played its part. A large tequila producer decided to launch an advertising campaign to uphold tequila as a national tradition, proclaiming that it was a good, healthy drink. Several plans were developed, and one was the production of a radio program called *Noches Tapatías*, a musical show that was so successful it was broadcast for well over twenty-five years.

*A flesh-and-blood cowboy
riding through agave plantations
on the outskirts of Tequila.*

141

"I wanted to forget
the way they do in Jalisco,
but those mariachis
and the tequila
only made me cry."

Portrait of José Alfredo Jiménez
by Emiliano Gironella.

"Ella," by José Alfredo Jiménez

The plant continues to flower • Jorge Negrete and Pedro Infante died, but their followers continued making movies and singing on the radio. "Mariachi Vargas," from Tecalitlán, became an example of the many routine contradictions when his mariachi costume had to be changed to look like a *charro* cowboy costume, because it worked better under lights.[30] Among the composers who continued to follow this established path were Ernesto Cortázar, Manuel Esperón, Cuco Sánchez, Tomás Méndez, Pepe Guizar, and many more. José Alfredo Jiménez played a special role. He wrote heartfelt songs that not only mentioned tequila but promoted the need to drink it in order to drown one's sorrows, remember a lost love, defy death, or forget. Another renowned singer was Lola Beltrán, also referred to as "Lola La Grande." As actors she and José Alfredo Jiménez, her love interest in many movies, were at best mediocre. However, Lola had a wonderful voice, and although José Alfredo wasn't strictly a singer, he had an emotional style that moved his audience. People flocked to their movies.

The Soler brothers were also briefly involved in this medium, though they disappeared quickly, one by one. The brother who had the greatest impact was Don Andrés. He appeared in movies in which everyone drank tequila in Technicolor, on horses or in sports cars, with brunettes in the mountains or beautiful blondes in luxurious mansions on Lake Chapala.

Art • Many murals, paintings, and sculptures have been made in which tequila appears, although in most cases they were the work of tequila producers who wanted to strengthen their corporate images.

In the large distilleries located around Tequila, one can find interesting murals. These works portray the ancient myths surrounding Mayahuel and other images of the indigenous past. They also depict some of the old haciendas, the original

"Man proposes, God disposes, the devil arrives and decomposes"

distilleries, portraits of the proprietors, or scenes of the Indians and *mestizos* laboring in the fields. There are sculptures of important personalities in the world of tequila, men such as Don Cenobio Sauza and Don José Cuervo.

In the vast collections of old tequila labels owned by Sauza and Cuervo

Typical image of traditional Mexican life featuring the classic drink on a José Cuervo publicity poster.

are some fascinating works of art. These evolved from the competition among tequila producers, whose only way of advertising their wares was by means of an arresting label. They were sometimes naive, but often brilliant. Tequila inspired artistic talent that goes far beyond the need to advertise.

After the labels came the so-called calendars, which are really posters. The originals were oil paintings on canvas that were then mass-produced. They portray the circumstances that surround tequila drinking: cock fighting, breaking in a horse, a young man giving flowers to a lady, and the inevitable *charro* cowboy scenes. In all of these posters there appears a beautiful woman, modest but showing a little cleavage, dressed in traditional Mexican clothes—the Jalisco costume is frequently used. The "tequila woman" looked chaste and shy, as befitted the women of the 1940s and 1950s. The men were always elegant and robust. In these posters both sexes are portrayed with white skin like the people from Los Altos, or slightly darker skin like those from Tapatío. It goes without saying, there is always a bottle of tequila present.

*The other side of the coin:
an allegorical float in the May 1
parade, Arandas, Jalisco.*

145

Tequila with everything •

When a Mexican man serenades the woman he loves or one who won't say yes, or even one who has given herself to him completely, it is unthinkable that he does it without tequila. It keeps him from playing out of tune and from catching cold. It also consoles him if the woman doesn't choose to come to the window, or he wishes to take revenge: *"He likes fighting cocks / he likes tequila, / but what he likes most / is breaking hearts."*

In many parts of Mexico, the cloudy, cool afternoons are called *tequileras*. When an afternoon is *tequilera*, one stays at home with friends or a good book, with a guitar nearby. It's an ideal moment for a smooth *añejo* and a Havana cigar.

"Once I dreaded tequila but now it's all I drink In each glass I see sorrow, in every sorrow I see a wish."

¡Hi ja jai! Like tequila, mariachis are indefatigable travelers from Jalisco who have become known around the world.

One may also spend these afternoons at a cantina, sipping tequila with the old gang and recalling good times while listening to the Yucatecan songs of Guty Cárdenas or Ricardo Palmerín. Then again, one may head for a trendy bar in the old barrio of San Angel in Mexico City and savor a glass of Real or Selección Suprema or a D'Antaño while Scott Joplin is played on the piano.

146

"Drunk from tequila, I carry drunkenness in my soul,
to see if I can heal this cruel melancholy."

During the month of September, when the whole country—houses, cars, stores, even the food—is decked out in red, white, and green,[31] tequila makes the rounds. On September 15, during the ceremony of El Grito (the Cry of Independence), all Mexico sings. In Zacatecas, Genaro Godina's march is sung; in Oaxaca it's Sandunga; in Veracruz we have the Colás; and in Guanajuato they sing the songs of José Alfredo Jiménez.

All kinds of gastronomic combinations are possible: Michoacan *carnitas* can be found in Tabasco; Yucatecan *papadzules* in Coahuila; Sinaloan *chilorio* in Chiapas; Guerrero green *pozole* in Baja California; Hidalgo soup with nuts and *chipotle* chile in Campeche; Puebla *mole* in Chihuahua; Nayarit chicken in mango sauce in Querétaro; Tamaulipas marinated oysters in Tlaxcala . . . it goes on and on. For these few days the boundaries are blurred, and though it's only September, for tequila it's Christmas.

There is nothing like tequila for mourning a lost love:

"I wanted to forget, the way they do in Jalisco
but those mariachis and the tequila
only made me cry."

"Ella," by José Alfredo Jiménez

A folkloric mural adorning a street in Arenal, Jalisco.

And, for betrayal:

"Who in this life is not familiar
with the well-known betrayal
that follows a sad love affair?
Who does not then go to the cantina
demanding a tequila,
and demanding a song?"

"Tu recuerdo y yo," by José Alfredo Jiménez

And, for romantic adventures, two tequilas, please:

"She said to me, 'Turn at the corner, we'll go to my house;
after a couple of tequilas we'll see what happens.'"

"Historia del taxi," by Ricardo Arjona

Or for a visitor in a new environment:

"Men get drunk on 'cucarachas.'
There is fire in some of the ladies' eyes . . .
Señorita, please bring a bottle of tequila
since it's so hot!
This life's so peaceful
that I shall get drunk in your honor."

"Mexico," by David Summers

For Mexican youth, rap music is a solemn requiem composed to put an end to the vulgarities of the world . . . but not to tequila:

"We went to the blast early
and we found my brother, Ramón.
He passed me his beer,
exclaiming: 'What a great party!'
There we met some chicks
who were neither 10's nor 2's
and we told them to line up
and serve us some tequila."

"Más vale cholo, rap o hip-hop," by Molotov

Finally, for the new generations who sing sensually of tequila though they may not actually drink it, we conclude with Thalia, one of today's biggest television stars, and her love for what is Mexican:

"Love, Mexican style, is cumbia, huapango and son,
horse, boots and a big hat, tequila, tobacco and rum.
Love, Mexican style, is the hot rhythm under the sun,
nice and slow, until some macho breaks my heart."

"Amor a la mexicana," by Mario Pupparo

The world of tequila is full of contradictions. It is true that advertising created false images, but then they became true again because people wished to believe in them. It's also true that tequila is a drink for day laborers, longshoremen, ditch diggers, bricklayers, and outcasts, but it's also a drink for the elite. Its residues contaminate rivers, but the same residues are good for the soil.

It's true that tequila was created to make Mexicans drunk and let loose the three demons within—the Indian, the Spaniard, and the *mestizo*—to flash sword, machete, or knife and tear each other apart while breath remains in their bodies. But it's also tequila, with or without mariachis, which has helped to liberate three other spirits—Quetzalcoatl, Jesus Christ, and the Virgin of Guadalupe—spirits that have caused these same Mexicans to build cathedrals, airports, cities, and hydroelectric plants, or to create symphonies, poetry, *huapangos,* and all the other glories of the Mexican nation.

"I'm sitting in the corner of a cantina

listening to the song I requested.

Now they're serving my tequila

and my thoughts find their way to you."

Salud! brand ratings, best bars, cocktails, and dishes

If you want to join the growing throng of well-informed tequila drinkers the world over, perhaps the tips that follow will help you achieve the greatest enjoyment with, we hope, the least embarrassment. We say "least embarrassment" because tequila aficionados are a fierce lot; your favorite brand may be someone else's battery acid. You don't believe it?

Just access "tequila" on the Internet and stand back. On the following pages we offer a professional rating of more than 100 of the top brands exported from Mexico, selected and ranked for us by the Sociedad Mexicana de Tequiliers (SMT; the Mexican Tequila Society), a group formed in 1993 and headquartered in Cancun. Their selections are the result of information gathering and professional tastings made by experts from a number of countries. Since all authentic tequila originates in Mexico, we consider SMT to be the most reliable source available. The brands are ranked from one to five stars, with only five labels reaching tequila heaven. We mention them now, in alphabetical order, for safety: José Cuervo's Reserva de la Familia, Herradura's Selección Suprema, 7 Leguas' Patrón, Tapatío's Paradiso, and Tequileña's Suave Patria Premium, all *añejos*.

Don't expect to become an expert on a shoestring budget. Good tequila is no longer cheap; the worldwide boom has seen to that. Still, there are a number of good two-star candidates, as our ratings show. We include a very few one-star brands, only because they are hugely successful, and to leave them out would be unfair. Any tequila that appears on the list is, in our opinion, "acceptable," and while most of them are available (although sometimes hard to locate) in Mexico, all of these brands can be bought in the United States and many in the United Kingdom and the rest of Europe. There are hundreds of tequila labels found around the world that have never seen the light of day in Mexico. Most of these are export names for absolutely authentic Mexican products, but a few are simply fraudulent.

Tequila facts and figures

But where to find the best tequilas? We've chosen a variety of major cities and listed a few of the bars and restaurants that make tequila a specialty; dazzling choices, super premiums, fantasy margaritas, and —very important—places that feature a barperson who knows what's what. Dozens of brands to choose from, often hundreds, all at your service from $3.50 a shot to $29.50 a snifter.

Many bars and many cities have been left out for reasons of space, but let us know your favorites, or send us a blast by e-mail if you disagree with our ratings or bar selections, and tell us why (revi@internet.com.mx).

Judge our ratings, enjoy our tequila bars, test our cocktail recipes and the surprising dishes cum tequila that you will find at the end of the chapter. But don't lean too heavily on our choices. The magic of tequila, like the magic of wine, is in the mind, body, and soul of the beholder—you. Salud!

1998 figures from the Council for the Regulation of Tequila (CRT) in Mexico show how well the U.S. market has been penetrated, but also how much work lies ahead in the rest of the world. Of the approximately 87,000,000 liters exported in that year, the United States represents 80%, Europe 13.5%, Latin America 3.5%, and the rest of the world 3%.

The top ten countries, in terms of liters of tequila received in 1998, are:

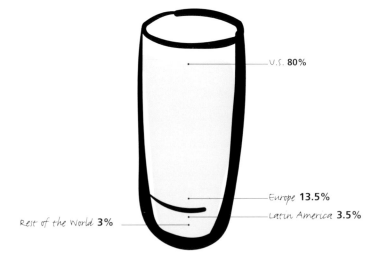

U.S. 80%
Europe 13.5%
Latin America 3.5%
Rest of the World 3%

U.S.	69,300,000
Germany	3,000,000
Holland	2,400,000
Belgium	1,800,000
France	1,800,000
Canada	1,000,000
Chile	1,000,000
U.K.	600,000
Japan	600,000
Spain	500,000

Despite the fact that the premium tequila segment has been the fastest growing in the alcoholic beverage industry in the United States, most of the brands sold are of the mixed variety. Of the approximately 250 brands widely available, the top five sellers have usually been:

Cuervo Especial	gold
Sauza	gold & white
Montezuma	gold
Pepe López	gold & white
Sauza Giro	white

All of these are imported in bulk and bottled in the U.S. and are in the $7–$20 range. Such 51/49% mixed brands make up 90% of the number of cases sold and are usually poured into margaritas, the best-selling cocktail in the United States. The remaining 10%—the upscale pure agave tequilas—contribute a surprising 25% of the total dollar volume. Upwardly mobile Anglo urbanites have been creating, then expanding, the premium and super premium market. There are now bottles being offered at Neiman-Marcus for up to $1,000 a pop. Like many trends, this is a California-driven phenomenon, although Florida, New York, and Illinois are now sipping their share of these expensive brands. The top five premium labels, normally but not always 100% agave *reposados* and *añejos*, include the following, which sell for $25–$60:

Sauza Hornitos	reposado
Sauza Conmemorativo	añejo
Patrón	añejo
Herradura	reposado & añejo
Cuervo 1800	añejo

Another enormous influence on the market, the 20,000,000-strong Mexican-American population, prefers 100% agave *reposados*, many of which, such as Cazadores and Jimador, are purchased in Mexico. Contrary to popular belief, other Hispanic groups such as Cubans and Puerto Ricans do not drink tequila any more than non-Hispanics.

What astute and responsible Mexican distillers want to communicate to the world is that, when made from 100% agave, tequila is one of the world's finest drinks, and that its palatable subtleties make it as nuanced and complex as expensive cognacs and single-malt whiskeys.

Advice from

Advice from tequila experts · Today, without a doubt, tequila is in vogue the world over, but to enjoy it fully one must learn how to select, taste, and evaluate this subtle liquid.

What tequila to ask for · There are four different types:

Joven, blanco, reposado, and añejo

How to tell one from the other

Tequila joven (*young*): this is also called "gold" and is usually a mixture of 51 percent agave and 49 percent other sugars, aged less than two months before bottling and often with a light amber color. Also called *abocado* (mild). Use a *caballito* (tequila shot glass).

Tequila blanco (*white*): also referred to as "silver," *blanco* is homogenized and bottled immediately after the completion of the double distillation process. This is the most common type but can be of very high quality. If drunk straight, a *caballito* is normally used.

Tequila reposado (*rested*): aged between two months and one year in white oak or pine barrels. Normally at least 80 percent agave. If taken straight, use a cordial or sherry glass.

Tequila añejo (*aged*): usually 100 percent agave, and aged in small white oak casks or barrels for at least one year, but as long as the distiller decides. There are *añejos* that are bottled after aging three, four, or five years. The most subtle and sophisticated of the four types, and often the most expensive. Sipped straight, using a brandy snifter.

How not to drink tequila

A major misapprehension among newcomers to tequila is that it should be drunk straight—"down the hatch"—in the old macho style. That's history. Now quality has improved so much that even the less expensive labels deserve to be savored.

a Tequilier

Here's how

The best way to discover which tequila suits your palate is to test by taste, always using a brandy snifter and following these steps:

1. Holding the glass at the base, raise it to eye level and study the color and body of the liquid, looking for clarity.

2. Swirl gently to the left for about one minute, and note whether the tequila clings to the sides of the glass, falling slowly to form a clear "string of pearls." If it does, start awarding stars.

3. After swirling the tequila, place your nose just above the rim of the glass and inhale deeply, searching for the full, rich, and slightly startling bouquet—almost a jolt.

4. Take a small sip, keeping it between your lips and the tip of the tongue for several seconds, relishing the first taste before swallowing.

5. Repeat this several times, swishing the tequila around the inside of your mouth before swallowing to give your taste buds a chance to enjoy and evaluate the subtleties that the makers have worked so long and hard to develop.

How to choose a tequila

Since there are so many brands on the market, each offering several options, it is not easy to make an informed choice. For this reason, what follows is a description of the subtle differences you may expect to find at each quality level, represented by one to five stars (★), along with the approximate retail price, in U.S. dollars,* of a .75-liter bottle. In the ratings of more than 100 of the top brands exported from Mexico, each is listed by type, brand name, NOM (the official identification code), distiller, average cost in the U.S. for a .75-liter bottle, average cost for a normal 1.5–2 oz. serving, and star rating as determined by the Sociedad Mexicana de Tequiliers.

Tip: look for the bargains—cost per star is a quick way of getting the most for your money.

*Note: To find approximate value in pounds Sterling divide by 1.60.

Quality levels

Description	Classification	Price (in U.S. dollars)
Standard essence of the tequila mescal plant with mixed taste of agave and sugar. Intense aroma. Unsubtle. Aggressive finish.	★	7.00–15.00
Acceptable "character" (the term used when the alcohol vapor releases a scent into one's nose) with agreeable agave taste and hints of wood, herbs, citrus, and other fruit.	★ ★	16.00–30.00
Balanced character, differentiated flavors, depending on the distillers' peculiarities. Definitive agave taste; strong presence of wood, wild herbs, fruit.	★ ★ ★	31.00–50.00
Very smooth and pleasant to the palate, with clean taste, wood smoke (oak or pine), traces of wild herbs, citrus, and oak.	★ ★ ★ ★	51.00–65.00
Completely balanced, great character, long finish. Contains all of above wood, herb, citrus, and other fruit essences. One hundred percent agave. Usually dark amber color. Five stars rarely awarded to anything but tequila *añejo*. Experts say it is "dressed in tails."	★ ★ ★ ★ ★	66.00–400.00

Note: It is important to try to evaluate tequila by taste test, not by price, since often a very acceptable tequila can be purchased at a surprisingly low cost.

The blue agave is an aloe—a healing plant in the lily family—and it has the highest concentration of fructose (as opposed to sucrose) sugars of any plant. It produces one of the healthiest of alcoholic beverages because the energy content is more readily absorbed and utilized by the body— good news for hangover sufferers.

Añejos

NAME	NOM	DISTILLER	Per 750 ml bottle (unless otherwise stated)	Per serving of 1.5 to 2.0 oz.	RATING
Herradura Selección Suprema	1119	Tequila Herradura	389.00	29.50	★ ★ ★ ★ ★
Cuervo Reserva de la Familia	1122	Casa Cuervo	75.00	10.50	★ ★ ★ ★ ★
Paradiso: El Tesoro de Don Felipe	1139	Tequila Tapatío	119.00	12.50	★ ★ ★ ★ ★
Suave Patria Premium	1146	Tequileña	65.00	15.00	★ ★ ★ ★ ★
Patrón	1120	Tequila 7 Leguas	53.00	6.50	★ ★ ★ ★ ★
1921 Reserva	1079	Agave Tequilana	83.00	5.00	★ ★ ★ ★
Herradura	1119	Tequila Herradura	59.00	6.50	★ ★ ★ ★
Cuervo 1800	1122	Casa Cuervo	51.00	7.50	★ ★ ★ ★
Gran Centenario	1122	Casa Cuervo	20.00	7.50	★ ★ ★ ★
Chinaco	1127	Tequilera La Gonzaleña	53.00	7.00	★ ★ ★ ★
El Tesoro de Don Felipe	1139	Tequila Tapatío	45.00	6.50	★ ★ ★ ★
Centinela	1140	Tequila Centinela	38.00	6.50	★ ★ ★ ★
Centinela Tres Años	1140	Tequila Centinela	63.00	6.50	★ ★ ★ ★
Suave Patria	1146	Tequileña	31.00	7.50	★ ★ ★ ★
Porfidio	(*)	Destilería Porfidio	60.00	6.00	★ ★ ★
Porfidio Cactus Bottle	(*)	Destilería Porfidio	70.00	8.00	★ ★ ★
Porfidio Single Barrel	(*)	Destilería Porfidio	80.00	15.00	★ ★ ★
Sauza Conmemorativo	1102	Tequila Sauza	28.00	5.00	★ ★ ★
Sauza Tres Generaciones	1102	Tequila Sauza	45.00	6.00	★ ★ ★
Pueblo Viejo	1103	Tequila San Matías de Jalisco	35.00	5.00	★ ★ ★
Centenario	1104	Tequila Cuervo La Rojeña	45.00	6.00	★ ★ ★
El Conquistador	1107	Tequila El Viejito	37.00	5.00	★ ★ ★
El Viejito	1107	Tequila El Viejito	35.00	5.00	★ ★ ★
Arette	1109	Destiladora Azteca de Jalisco	52.00	8.50	★ ★ ★
Alcatraz	1110	Tequila Orendáin de Jalisco	52.00	8.50	★ ★ ★
Don Julio Reserva	1118	Tequila Tres Magueyes	42.00	6.00	★ ★ ★
Lápiz	1146	Tequileña	49.00	6.50	★ ★ ★
Casta	1173	Tequila Newton e Hijos	89.00	11.00	★ ★ ★
Corralejo	1368	Tequilera Corralejo	45.00	6.00	★ ★ ★
Porfidio Blue	(*)	Destilería Porfidio	40.00	6.50	★ ★
Jalisciense	1068	Agroindustrial Guadalajara	30.00	5.00	★ ★
Sauza Conmemorativo (mixto)	1102	Tequila Sauza	20.00	4.50	★ ★
Sauza Tres Generaciones (mixto)	1102	Tequila Sauza	33.00	5.50	★ ★
Sauza Triada	1102	Tequila Sauza	43.00	6.00	★ ★
Reserva del Dueño	1107	Tequila El Viejito	38.00	6.00	★ ★
Real Hacienda	1111	Tequila Viuda de Romero	36.00	6.00	★ ★
Herencia	1124	Tequilas del Señor	36.00	6.00	★ ★
Río de Plata	1124	Tequilas del Señor	35.00	6.50	★ ★

(*) Porfidio brands have been distilled by several different companies. Thus labels show corresponding NOM codes.

There are 66 certified distilleries in Mexico that produce 508 brands. In addition, there are some 180 brands authorized to be bottled outside of Mexico by registered users that use their own labels provided they always print the NOM code of the original manufacturer.

Reposados

NAME	NOM	DISTILLER	Per 750 ml bottle (unless otherwise stated)	Per serving of 1.5 to 2.0 oz.	RATING
Hussong's	1107	Tequila El Viejito	24.00	5.50	★ ★ ★ ★
Don Julio	1118	Tequila Tres Magueyes	40.00	6.50	★ ★ ★ ★
Suave Patria Red Label	1146	Tequileña	21.00	4.00	★ ★ ★ ★
La Cava de Don Agustín Reserva	1131	La Arandina	40.00	6.50	★ ★ ★
Gusano Real	1173	Tequilera Newton e Hijos	65.00	11.50	★ ★ ★
1921 Reserva	1079	Agave Tequilana	45.00	9.50	★ ★ ★
Sauza Galardón	1102	Tequila Sauza	28.00	6.00	★ ★ ★
Sauza Hornitos	1102	Tequila Sauza	26.00	5.00	★ ★ ★
Pueblo Viejo	1103	Tequila San Matías de Jalisco	27.00	4.50	★ ★ ★
San Matías	1103	Tequila San Matías de Jalisco	40.00	4.00	★ ★ ★
Centenario	1104	Tequila Cuervo La Rojeña	40.00	5.50	★ ★ ★
El Conquistador	1107	Tequila El Viejito	36.00	4.50	★ ★ ★
El Viejito	1107	Tequila El Viejito	22.00	4.00	★ ★ ★
Arette	1109	Destiladora Azteca de Jalisco	36.00	6.50	★ ★ ★
Alteño	1111	Tequila Viuda de Romero	35.00	5.00	★ ★ ★
Viuda de Romero	1111	Tequila Viuda de Romero	25.00	4.50	★ ★ ★
Misión Imperial	1115	Tequila La Parreñita	22.00	4.00	★ ★ ★
El Jimador	1119	Tequila Herradura	30.00	5.00	★ ★ ★
Herradura	1119	Tequila Herradura	45.00	5.50	★ ★ ★
Cuervo Tradicional	1122	Casa Cuervo	28.00	4.50	★ ★ ★
Chinaco	1127	Tequilera La Gonzaleña	51.00	6.50	★ ★ ★
Cazadores	1128	Tequila Cazadores	32.00	5.50	★ ★ ★
Tenoch	1137	La Cofradía	40.00	7.00	★ ★ ★
El Tesoro de Don Felipe	1139	Tequila Tapatío	43.00	6.00	★ ★ ★
Centinela	1140	Tequila Centinela	38.00	6.00	★ ★ ★
Lápiz	1146	Tequileña	41.00	7.50	★ ★ ★
Las Trancas	1146	Tequileña	45.00	5.00	★ ★ ★
Corralejo	1368	Tequilera Corralejo	34.00	6.00	★ ★ ★
Tres Mujeres	1258	J. Jesús Partida Meléndrez	18.00	5.50	★ ★
Los Valientes	740	Indust. Desarrollo Sto. Tomás	28.00	6.50	★ ★
Porfidio	(*)	Destilería Porfidio	41.00	7.00	★ ★
Alcatraz	1110	Tequila Orendáin de Jalisco	29.00	5.00	★ ★
Real Hacienda	1111	Tequila Viuda de Romero	29.00	5.00	★ ★
Revolución	1112	Tequila Santa Fe	32.00	5.50	★ ★
Cinco de Mayo	1119	Tequila Herradura	30.00	6.00	★ ★
Gran Centenario	1122	Casa Cuervo	45.00	5.50	★ ★
Herencia	1124	Tequilas del Señor	35.00	6.00	★ ★
Casta Brava (1 liter)	1173	Tequilera Newton e Hijos	26.00	4.50	★ ★
Casta Oro	1173	Tequilera Newton e Hijos	34.00	6.00	★ ★
El Charro	1235	Tequilera Rústica de Arandas	21.00	3.50	★ ★
Sierra Brava (1 liter)	1298	Tequila Sierra Brava	30.00	5.00	★ ★
Los Arango	1368	Tequilera Corralejo	40.00	7.00	★ ★
Casa Noble	1137	La Cofradía	50.00	9.00	★ ★
Casa Noble Crystal	1137	La Cofradía	43.00	7.50	★ ★

(*) Porfidio brands have been distilled by several different companies. Thus labels show corresponding NOM codes.

silver or white

NAME	NOM	DISTILLER	Per 750 ml bottle (unless otherwise stated)	Per serving of 1.5 to 2.0 oz.	RATING
Herradura	1119	Tequila Herradura	35.00	4.50	★ ★ ★ ★
El Tesoro de Don Felipe	1139	Tequila Tapatío	41.00	5.50	★ ★ ★ ★
Porfidio	(*)	Destilería Porfidio	60.00	6.00	★ ★ ★
Porfidio Cactus Bottle	(*)	Destilería Porfidio	60.00	10.00	★ ★ ★
Porfidio Triple Distilled	(*)	Destilería Porfidio	55.00	9.00	★ ★ ★
1921	1079	Agave Tequilana	74.00	4.50	★ ★ ★
1921 Reserva Especial	1079	Agave Tequilana	49.00	8.50	★ ★ ★
1921 Single Barrel	1079	Agave Tequilana	45.00	7.50	★ ★ ★
Centenario	1104	Tequila Cuervo La Rojeña	33.00	5.00	★ ★ ★
Distinqt Platinum	1107	Tequila El Viejito	49.00	8.50	★ ★ ★
El Viejito	1107	Tequila El Viejito	45.00	7.50	★ ★ ★
Pepe López	1110	Tequila Orendáin de Jalisco	9.00	3.50	★ ★ ★
Don Julio	1118	Tequila Tres Magueyes	38.00	5.50	★ ★ ★
Patrón	1120	Tequila 7 Leguas	47.00	6.00	★ ★ ★
Porfidio Blue	(*)	Destilería Porfidio	39.00	6.50	★ ★
Porfidio Single Barrel	(*)	Destilería Porfidio	59.00	10.00	★ ★
Sauza	1102	Tequila Sauza	11.00	4.00	★ ★
Pueblo Viejo	1103	Tequila San Matías de Jalisco	23.00	4.00	★ ★
San Matías	1103	Tequila San Matías de Jalisco	21.00	3.50	★ ★
El Conquistador	1107	Tequila El Viejito	29.00	4.00	★ ★
Reserva del Dueño	1107	Tequila El Viejito	33.00	5.50	★ ★
Arette	1109	Destiladora Azteca de Jalisco	29.00	5.00	★ ★
Alcatraz	1110	Tequila Orendáin de Jalisco	29.00	5.00	★ ★
Cinco de Mayo	1119	Tequila Herradura	22.00	6.00	★ ★
El Jimador	1119	Tequila Herradura	22.00	4.00	★ ★
Dos Reales	1122	Casa Cuervo	20.00	5.00	★ ★
Gran Centenario	1122	Casa Cuervo	38.00	5.50	★ ★
Herencia	1124	Tequilas del Señor	35.00	6.00	★ ★
Chinaco	1127	Tequilera La Gonzaleña	49.00	6.00	★ ★
Centinela	1140	Tequila Centinela	47.00	5.50	★ ★
Montezuma	1143	Destiladora González González	8.00	3.50	★ ★
Lápiz Platinum	1146	Tequileña	39.00	5.50	★ ★
Sauza Giro (1 liter)	1102	Tequila Sauza	7.00	4.00	★
Cuervo	1122	Casa Cuervo	11.00	3.50	★

(*) Porfidio brands have been distilled by several different companies. Thus labels show corresponding NOM codes.

Gold

NAME	NOM	DISTILLER	Per 750 ml bottle (unless otherwise stated)	Per serving of 1.5 to 2.0 oz.	RATING
Pepe López	1110	Tequila Orendáin de Jalisco	10.00	3.50	★ ★ ★
Viuda de Romero	1111	Tequila Viuda de Romero	20.00	4.00	★ ★ ★
Herradura	1119	Tequila Herradura	36.00	5.00	★ ★ ★
Patrón	1120	Tequila 7 Leguas	55.00	8.50	★ ★ ★
Cuervo 1800 (mixto)	1122	Casa Cuervo	34.00	5.00	★ ★ ★
Lápiz	1146	Tequileña	50.00	8.00	★ ★ ★
Sauza Extra	1102	Tequila Sauza	10.00	3.50	★ ★
El Toro	1110	Tequila Orendáin de Jalisco	8.00	3.50	★ ★
Matador (1 liter)	1122	Casa Cuervo	10.00	3.50	★ ★
El Grito	1137/1142	La Cofradía or La Madrileña	21.00	4.50	★ ★
Two Fingers	1142	La Madrileña	15.00	4.00	★ ★
Montezuma	1143	Destiladora González González	8.00	3.50	★ ★
Sauza	1102	Tequila Sauza	14.00	4.00	★
Sauza Giro (1 liter)	1102	Tequila Sauza	7.00	4.00	★
Cuervo Especial (1 liter)	1122	Casa Cuervo	15.00	4.50	★
Cuervo Gold	1122	Casa Cuervo	14.00	4.00	★

Sauza is the second largest tequila distiller. In many ways, this firm was responsible for the big industry modernization after World War II. Although they are not yet in the super premium range, the quality of their products has always been consistent. According to some experts from the United States, Sauza Hornitos might be the best of all the 100 percent agave reposados since it is excellent straight and the best choice for a margarita.

൭൭

Tequila Cuervo is by far the largest (up to 73 million liters/year) and oldest (over 200 years) distillery. Their brand Cuervo Gold (in different presentations), although it is not a 100 percent agave tequila, is the most popular around the world.

The shot heard 'round the world

Tequila is in boom time. Hundreds of tequila bars open every year, from Stellenbosch to Bassersdorf, from Singapore to downtown Moscow.

But the United States is still the "T" drinker's paradise, and in the listings below you will find this country represented in the approximate proportion that its tequila consumption merits.

You'll find countries listed alphabetically, along with states (where needed), cities, and then the names, addresses, and telephone numbers of a few score bars and restaurants that our tireless researchers have uncovered. All feature an exorbitant number of brands, most will offer a variety of margaritas to exhaust your imagination, and each and every one specializes in the new, delicious, expensive (but worth it) super premiums. Many have mariachi music on selected nights, and fantasy Mexican "ambientes"; you should telephone first to find out what's happening and to make reservations if needed.

Where it's happening

COUNTRY	CITY	NAME	ADDRESS & TEL. NO.
AUSTRALIA	Melbourne	Tequila Blues	493 Chapel St., South Yarra, Melbourne. Tel.: (03) 9827-0830
		Tequila Sunrise Fresh Pty Ltd.	2/22 Kylie Pl., Cheltenham, Melbourne. Tel.: (03) 9555-7477
	Sydney	New Tequila Mexican Restaurant	260a South Tce, Bankstown, Sydney. Tel.: (02) 9790-5279
		Tequila Mexican Restaurant	200 Pittwater Rd., Manly, Sydney. Tel.: (02) 9977-0718
CANADA	Montreal	Cactus 4461	St-Denis, Montreal, Quebec. Tel.: (514) 849-0349
		Carlos & Pepe's	1420 Peel St., Montreal, Quebec. Tel.: (514) 288-3090
		El Coyote Bar	1202 Bishop, Montreal, Quebec. Tel.: (514) 875-7082
	Vancouver	Las Margaritas Restaurant & Cantina	West 4th Ave., Vancouver, B.C. Tel.: (604) 734-7117
FRANCE	Paris	Tequila Bar	Centre Commercial "Les 4 Temps," Rue des Arcades, Niveau 0, 92800 PUTEAUX. Tel.: (1) 4778-40571999
GERMANY	Berlin	Locus	Marheinikeplatz 4, U-7 Gneisenaustr., Berlin. Tel.: (30) 691-5637
		Tres Kilos	Marheinikeplatz 3, U-7 Gneisenaustr., Berlin. Tel.: (30) 693-6044
ITALY	Rome	El Tropico Latino	Via Mazzini 77/a. Tel.: (6) 335932
JAPAN	Tokyo	Café Coyote	Daiba 1-3-3, Sunset Beach Restaurant Row, Tokyo. Tel.: (3) 5531-5007
		Fondo de la Madrugada	Jingumae 2-33-12-B2, Harajuku North, Tokyo. Tel.: 5410-6288
RUSSIA	Moscow	Azteca	11 ul. Novoslobodskaya, Moscow. Tel.: (095) 957-8467
SINGAPORE	Singapore	Margarita's	108 Faber Drive, Faber Garde, Singapore.
SOUTH AFRICA	Stellenbosch	Cantina Tequila	University Town.
SPAIN	Madrid	Don Pelayo	Alcalá 33, Madrid. Tel.: (1) 531-0031
		El Rincón Azteca	Príncipe de Vergara 78, Madrid. Tel.: (1) 411-6919
		La Misión	José Silva 22, Madrid. Tel.: (1) 519-2463
		Malpaso	Avenida de Europa 15, Centro Comercial La Moraleja, Madrid. Tel.: (1) 661-9095
		Sí Señor	Castellana 128, Madrid. Tel.: (1) 564-0604
		Tequila Sal y Limón	Castellana 95, Madrid. Tel.: (1) 556-9347
SWITZERLAND	Bassersdorf	Mexican Bar Tres Amigos	Winterthurerstrasse 1, 8303 Bassersdorf. Tel.: (01) 836-5200
	Zürich	Bar Pacífico	Limmatquai 70, 8001 Zürich. Tel.: (01) 252-6300
U.K.	London	Cactus Blue	86 Fulham Rd., London SW3. Tel.: (0171) 823-7858
		Che	23 St. James' St., London SW1. Tel.: (0171) 747-9380
		El Barco Latino	Temple Pier, Victoria Embankment, WC2. Tel.: (0171) 379-7496
		Texas Embassy Cantina	1 Cockspur St., London SW1. Tel.: (0171) 925-0077
		Texas Lone Star	154 Gloucester Rd., London SW7. Tel.: (0171) 370-5625
		Bar Rumba	41 High Street, London EN5. Tel.: (0181) 441-7236
		Navajo Joe	34 King Street, London WC2. Tel.: (0171) 240-4008
		Detroit Bar	30 Earlham Street, Covent Garden, London WC2. Tel.: (0171) 240-2662

U.S.A

STATE	CITY	NAME	ADDRESS & TEL. NO.
Arizona	Glendale	La Perla	5912 W. Glendale Ave. Tel.: (602) 939-7561
		Macayo's	4001 N. Central. Tel.: (602) 264-6141
	Paradise Valley	Garcia's	4924 E. Shea Blvd. Tel.: (602) 367-0220
	Phoenix	Garcia's	Del Metro Shopping Center, 3301 W. Peoria Ave. Tel.: (602) 866-1850
		Garcia's	2212 N. 35th Ave. Tel.: (602) 272-5584
	Scottsdale	Los Olivos	7328 E. 2nd St. Tel.: (602) 946-2256
California	Burlingame	Left at Albuquerque	1100 Burlingame Ave. Tel.: (650) 401-5700
	Concorde	La Tapatía Mexican Restaurant & Cantina	1802 Willow Pass Rd. Tel.: (510) 685-1985
	Encinitas	El Callejón	345 S. Coast Highway 101. Tel.: (760) 634-2793
	Long Beach	Tequila Jack's	Shoreline Drive. Tel.: (562) 628-0454
	Los Angeles	Casa Tequila	20923 Roscoe Blvd., Canoga Park. Tel.: (818) 341-8503
		Catalina Cantina	1701 S. Catalina Ave., Redondo Beach. Tel.: (310) 791-5440
		El Coyote	7312 Beverly Blvd. Tel.: (323) 939-2255
		El Cholo	1121 S. Western Ave. Tel.: (323) 734-2773
	Pleasanton	Blue Agave Club	625 Main St. Tel.: (510) 417-1224
	Sacramento	Los Nopales	106 J Street. Tel.: (916) 443-6376
	San Diego	El Agave	2304 San Diego Ave. Tel.: (619) 220-0692
		Old Town Mexican Café	2489 San Diego Ave. Tel.: (619) 297-4330
	San Francisco	Tommy's Restaurant	5929 Geary Blvd. Tel.: (415) 387-4747
Colorado	Denver	Las Margaritas	1035 E. 17th at Downing. Tel.: (303) 830-2199
		Las Margaritas	1066 Olde Gaylord St. Tel.: (303) 777-0194
Florida	Coral Gables	Tequila Sunrise	3894 SW 8th St. Tel.: (305) 446-8280
Illinois	Chicago	Don Juan's	6730 N. Northwest Highway.
		Frontera Grill	445 N. Clark St. Tel.: (312) 661-1434
		Hacienda Tecalitlan Restaurant	820 N. Ashland Ave. (betw. W. Fry St. and W. Chicago Ave.). Tel.: (312) 243-1166
		Salpicón	1252 N. Wells St. Tel.: (312) 988-7811
Louisiana	New Orleans	Superior Bar & Grill	3636 St. Charles. Tel.: (504) 899-4200
		Vaqueros	4938 Prytania. Tel.: (504) 891-6441
Maryland	Ocean City	Tequila Mockingbird	130th St. at Montego Bay Shopping Center

U.S.A

STATE	CITY	NAME	ADDRESS & TEL. NO.
Michigan	Detroit	Capt. Tony's Key West Bar & Grill	3335 N. Woodward Ave., Royal Oak. Tel.: (248) 288-6388
		Old Mexico Restaurant	5566 Drake Road, West Bloomfield Twp. Tel.: (248) 661-8088
		Prickly Pear Café	328 S. Main St., Ann Arbor. Tel.: (734) 930-0047
Minnesota	Minneapolis	Bar Abilene	1300 Lagoon Ave. (Fremont Ave. S. & Lagoon Ave.) Tel.: (612) 825-2525
	St. Paul	Boca Chica Restaurante	11 Concord St. (Humboldt Ave. & Concord St.) Tel.: (651) 222-8499
New Mexico	Santa Fe	Maria's New Mexican Kitchen	555 West Cordova. Tel.: (505) 983-7929
North Carolina	Willmington	Kiva Grill	Porter's Neck Shopping Center, 8211 Market St. Tel.: (910) 686-8211
New York	New York	Arizona 206	206 East 60th St. Tel.: (212) 838-0440
		El Rio Grande	160 E. 38th St. Tel.: (212) 867-0922
		Maya	1191 First Ave. (at 64th St.) Tel.: (212) 585-1818
		Mesa Grill	102 Fifth Ave. Tel.: (212) 807-7400
		Mi Cocina	57 Jane St. (at Hudson St.) Tel.: (212) 627-8273
		Session 73	1359 First Ave. (at 73rd St.) Tel.: (212) 517-4445
		Tapika	950 Eighth Ave., Manhattan Tel.: (212) 397-3737
		The Alamo	304 East 48th St. Tel.: (212) 759-0590
	Larchmont	Tequila Sunrise	145 Larchmont Ave. Tel.: (914) 834-6378
	Bayside	Tequila Sunrise	34-37 Bell Blvd. Tel.: (718) 631-0377
	Long Island City	Tequila Sunrise	40-01 Northern Blvd. Tel.: (718) 729-3301
	Roslyn Heights	Tequila Sunrise	388 Willis Ave. Tel.: (516) 484-3341
Pennsylvania	Philadelphia	Tequila's	1511 Locust. Tel.: (215) 546-0181
Texas	Austin	Iron Cactus	606 Trinity. Tel.: (512) 472-9240
	Dallas	Mattito's Café Mexicano	4311 Oak Lawn. Tel.: (214) 526-8181
	Fort Worth	Blue Mesa	1600 South University. Tel.: (817) 332-6372
	Houston	Las Alamedas on Post Oak	1800 Post Oak Blvd. (Post Oak at Ambassador). Tel.: (713) 965-9600
	San Antonio	Tequila Mockingbird at Presidio Plaza	245 East Commerce, Suite 101. Tel.: (210) 472-2265
	Webster	Pinche's Tequila Grill	20235 Gulf Freeway. (betw. Bay Area Blvd. and NASA Rd. 1). Tel.: (281) 332-9416
Washington	Bellingham	Downtown Johnny's	1408 Cornwall Ave. Tel.: (360) 733-2579
	Seattle	El Niño	113 Virginia St. (near Pike Place Market). Tel.: (206) 441-5454
Washington, D.C.	Washington, D.C.	Tequila Grill	20th and K St. Tel.: (202) 833-3640

Tequila-based cocktails

Tequila cocktails are nothing new to the mixed drinks world, and we are happy to reproduce some old favorites. Nonetheless, we have also included a few surprises we think you should know about.

While we recommend following closely the suggested quantities and mixing instructions for each drink, don't be afraid to add a dash of your own inspiration for that personal touch. Also for best results, stick to the quality brands, remembering that taste, not price, should lead to the right tequila for each drink.

The Margarita Cocktail

By far the favorite tequila cocktail in the United States is the margarita. Its invention is attributed to a bartender, Francisco "Pancho" Morales. According to his obituary published by the Tequila Ministry,[32] he served his first margarita on July 4, 1942, in Ciudad Juárez, Chihuahua. Señor Morales died at age seventy-eight in January 1997. According to the ministry, which based its material on news agencies like Notimex and Reuters, Señor Morales was working in Tommy's Bar when a woman came in and named a cocktail he had never heard of. Like any good professional, he pretended to know and created a cocktail out of crushed ice, Cointreau, lime juice and tequila. The woman loved it and asked what the drink was called, and the margarita was born. Gabriel Morales, the son of the famous bartender, claims that his father never patented the drink and so never made a dime on his invention. As a matter of fact, Señor Morales emigrated to the United States, where he worked as a milkman for twenty-five years until he retired in 1981. Morales's son also claims that his father never bragged about his invention and never even liked it.

The Classic Margarita

1 1/2   ounces tequila *blanco* (white) ★ ★ ★ ★

3/4   ounce triple sec or Cointreau

1/2   ounce lime juice

    dash of syrup (unflavored)

Place all ingredients in the blender, together with crushed ice. Blend quickly. Serve in a large cocktail glass, salted around the rim, with a slice of lime and 2 short straws.

The Golden Margarita

1 1/2   ounces tequila *añejo* ★ ★ ★ ★

3/4   ounce Grand Marnier

1/2   ounce lime juice

Place all ingredients in the blender, together with crushed ice. Blend quickly. Serve in a cocktail glass, with a slice of lime and 2 short straws.

Strawberry Margarita

1 1/2   ounces tequila *blanco* (white) ★ ★ ★

3/4   ounce Cointreau or Triple Sec

1/2   ounce lime juice

3 1/2   ounces frozen or fresh strawberries

    dash of grenadine

Place all ingredients in the blender, together with crushed ice. Blend quickly. Serve in a cocktail glass decorated with a strawberry or lime slice and 2 short straws.

The classic margarita cocktail.

Mexican Breeze

1 1/2	ounces tequila *reposado* ★ ★ ★
4	ounces orange juice
1	ounce grapefruit juice
1	ounce pineapple juice
1/4	ounce lime juice
	dash of cherry liqueur

Place all the ingredients in a Collins glass with ice cubes, a slice of lime, and a long cocktail stick.

"Sleeping Woman" Tequila

1 1/2	ounces tequila *blanco* (white) ★ ★ ★ ★
2	ounces pineapple juice
1/4	ounce white crème de menthe
3 1/2	ounces *guanábana* (soursop) fruit

Place all the ingredients in a blender, together with crushed ice. Blend well. Serve in a cocktail or coupe glass, decorated with a pineapple slice and cherries and 2 short straws.

Submarine

| 2 | ounces tequila *reposado* ★ ★ ★ |
| | light beer to fill |

Fill a *caballito* (tequila shot) glass with tequila. Cover the *caballito* with an inverted glass, then turn upside down, holding the *caballito* inside. Fill the glass with the cold beer.

Martini Pique

2 1/2	ounces tequila *blanco* (white) ★ ★
	a few drops of dry vermouth
	grated rind of 1/2 a lime

Place all the ingredients in a cocktail shaker. Add 3 ice cubes and shake well. Serve in a cold martini glass and decorate with a jalapeño chile and 2 olives.

Left: *Martini Pique*
Right: *Ecological Bloody Mary*

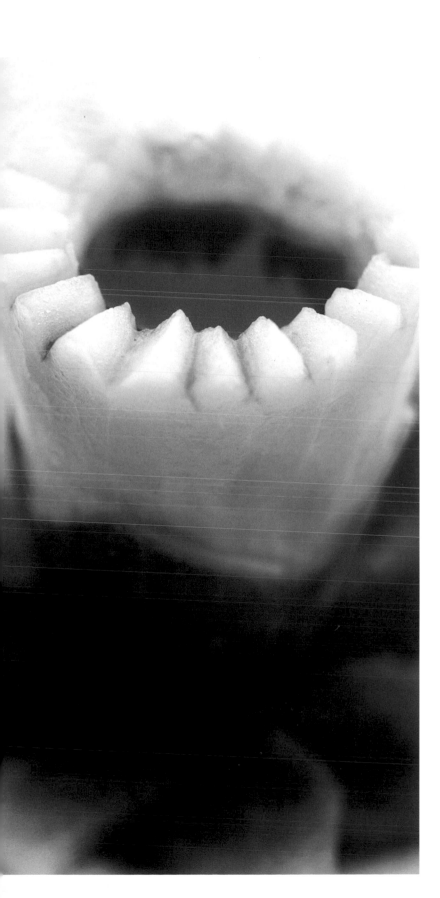

Ecological Bloody Mary

1   ounce tequila *blanco* (white) ★ ★ ★

3   ounces prepared *sangrita*

1/2   fresh cucumber, hollowed

Peel three-quarters of the cucumber, leaving the bottom quarter with skin. Hollow the cucumber.

For the classic, homemade *sangrita*, mix together tomato juice, lime juice, salt, pepper, Worcestershire sauce, Tabasco sauce, and orange juice to taste. Mix the tequila with the *sangrita* in a glass, then pour into the hollowed cucumber and decorate with a slice of watermelon and a straw.

Parraschino Cocktail

Original recipe of the famous Mexican architect Manuel Parra.

1   liter tequila *reposado* ★ ★ ★

1   handful of raisins

       orange peel cut in strips

       large bunch of spearmint leaves

1   stick of cinammon

Pour the liter of tequila *reposado* into a large flagon (with top), fill with spearmint leaves, and add remaining ingredients. Leave to stand for a minimum of 15 days or up to 2 months. Serve in *caballito* glasses.

Tequila Shot (Straight up)

2   ounces tequila *blanco* (white) ★ ★ ★

2   ounces prepared *sangrita*

Serve in separate *caballito* (tequila shot) glasses.

Maximilian's Tequila

1 1/2   ounces tequila *añejo* ★ ★ ★ ★ ★

3/4   ounce Napoleon mandarin liqueur

Place the ingredients directly into a brandy snifter. Serve with a soda chaser.

Highland Tequila

1 1/2   ounces tequila *añejo* ★ ★ ★ ★ ★

3/4   ounce Drambuie liqueur

Place the ingredients in an old-fashioned glass over ice cubes. Serve with short cocktail stick.

Sombrero

1 1/2   ounces tequila *reposado* ★ ★ ★

3/4   ounce Kalhua coffee liqueur

3/4   ounce cream

Place tequila and cream in a blender and mix well. Serve together with the Kahlua in an old-fashioned glass.

Tequila Sunrise

1 1/2   ounces tequila *blanco* (white) ★ ★ ★

   orange juice to fill

   dash of grenadine

   dash of blackcurrant liqueur

Place all the ingredients in a highball glass on top of ice cubes and decorate with a slice of orange and cherries and a straw.

Ráfaga (or Gust of Wind)

1   ounce tequila *blanco* (white) ★ ★ ★

1/2   ounce green crème de menthe

1/2   ounce Xtabentún (sweet anise liqueur)

Place all ingredients without ice in a *caballito* (tequila shot) glass. Set alight and serve with a long straw.

Left: *Tequila Sunrise*

Mexico on Fire

1 1/2   ounces tequila *añejo* ★ ★ ★ ★
1/2   ounce Amaretto
   champagne to fill

Place all the ingredients in a champagne flute. Serve with a twist of orange peel and a red cherry.

Tequila "Jade"

1 1/2   ounces tequila *blanco* (white) ★ ★ ★
2   ounces Midori
1/2   ounce lime juice
3 1/2   ounces kiwi fruit

Place all the ingredients in a blender together with crushed ice. Blend. Serve in coupe glass, decorated with a slice of kiwi and 2 short straws.

Cucaracha

1   ounce tequila *blanco* (white) ★ ★ ★ ★
1/2   ounce Kalhua
1/2   ounce Cointreau

Place all the ingredients in a glass, without ice. Set alight and serve with a long straw. (The straw must be inserted immediately and the cocktail drunk straightaway.)

Mexico on Fire.

Tequila-based dishes

Heat the olive oil in a saucepan over a medium flame and when hot, sauté the onion until translucent; add the garlic. Raise the heat and add the mushrooms, salt, and pepper. Stir gently with a wooden spoon until cooked but still firm. Pour the tequila over and set alight, allowing the liquid to evaporate a little. Place on a serving dish.

For the *guajillo* chile rings: heat the 2 tablespoons of oil in a small frying pan over a high flame. Add the chile rings, stirring with a perforated spoon until crisp. Drain, add salt, and place on top of the mushrooms to serve.

Ceviche

(serves 6)

1 pound (1/2 kg) of *sierra* (mackerel), cleaned and cut into 1-inch cubes

1/2 cup of lime juice

1/4 cup of orange juice

1/2 cup of tequila, plus extra to sprinkle

2 tablespoons ketchup

14 ounces (400g) chopped tomato (without seeds)

3 tablespoons chopped onion

2 tablespoons finely chopped cilantro (coriander leaves)

2 tablespoons sliced canned jalapeño chiles, chopped

1 teaspoon dried oregano

1 1/2 teaspoons salt, or to taste

2 medium avocados, finely diced

2 tablespoons olive oil

Place the fish in a glass bowl and cover with the juices and the tequila. Cover with cling wrap and place in the lower part of the refrigerator for at least 3 hours, or until fish is

Mushrooms with guajillo chile

(serves 6)

4 tablespoons olive oil

2 tablespoons finely chopped onion

4 cloves garlic

1 pound (1/2 kg) of clean (not washed) sliced mushrooms

1 teaspoon salt

freshly ground pepper

4 tablespoons tequila

2 tablespoons oil

2 large *guajillo* chiles, cleaned and sliced into rings

opaque. Stir occasionally so all the fish "cooks."

Mix the fish carefully with the tomato, ketchup, onion, cilantro, chiles, oregano, and one of the avocados, adding salt and olive oil. Place the remaining avocado on top and sprinkle with some more tequila. Serve cold.

Salmon marinated in tequila

(serves 2)

2   slices of smoked salmon (2 ounces [60 g] each)

4   tablespoons tequila

    oil for final presentation

4   tablespoons diced, seedless tomato

2   tablespoons finely chopped spring onion

1   tablespoon finely chopped cilantro (coriander)

1   finely chopped *serrano* chile, without seeds
    (or to taste)

    salt

2   tablespoons refried beans

2   tostadas (fried tortillas), approx. 4 inches (10 cm) in
    diameter

1   bunch (5 ounces [150 g]) spinach leaves
    oil for deep frying and salt

In deep individual dishes, marinate each slice of salmon in 2 tablespoons of tequila; cover each dish with cling wrap and leave for 30 minutes. Carefully mix together the tomato, spring onion, coriander, chile, and salt to taste. Spread one spoon of refried beans on each tostada.

Wipe clean (but do not wash) the spinach leaves and chop them in 1/3-inch (1 cm) pieces. In a deep fryer, heat oil (approx. depth of 1 1/3 inches [4 cm]). When oil begins to smoke, plunge in the frying basket with the spinach. Stir occasionally with a perforated spoon. When the leaves are crisp—approx. 4 minutes—remove the basket and leave to drain. Then place spinach on absorbent paper and sprinkle with salt.

Presentation: On a flat dish, brush each slice of salmon lightly with oil. On individual plates, place the tostada spread with beans and half of the tomato mixture, top with the salmon slices, and on one side, place the fried spinach.

shrimp with julienne of orange

(serves 6)

24	medium-sized shrimp
	water
1	small onion, roughly chopped
2	cloves garlic
2	teaspoons salt
3	tablespoons butter
1	tablespoon finely chopped onion
2	*serrano* chiles, finely chopped
4	tablespoons julienne of orange
1/2	cup tequila
3	tablespoons finely chopped cilantro (coriander)

To make the julienne: with a potato peeler, cut very fine strips from the outer skin of the orange. Place the strips in a sieve and plunge first in boiling water, then immediately under cold running water. Repeat the procedure three times in order to remove the bitter taste. Pat the julienne dry with a paper towel.

To cook the shrimp: Place the water in a saucepan together with the onion, garlic, and salt and bring to the boil. Add the shrimp and cook until they turn a pink color. Drain well and clean.

Heat the butter in a frying pan over a high flame. Add the chopped onion and when translucent, add the shrimp and fry gently. Then add the chiles and the orange julienne. Flambé with the tequila, and finally, add the cilantro and salt.

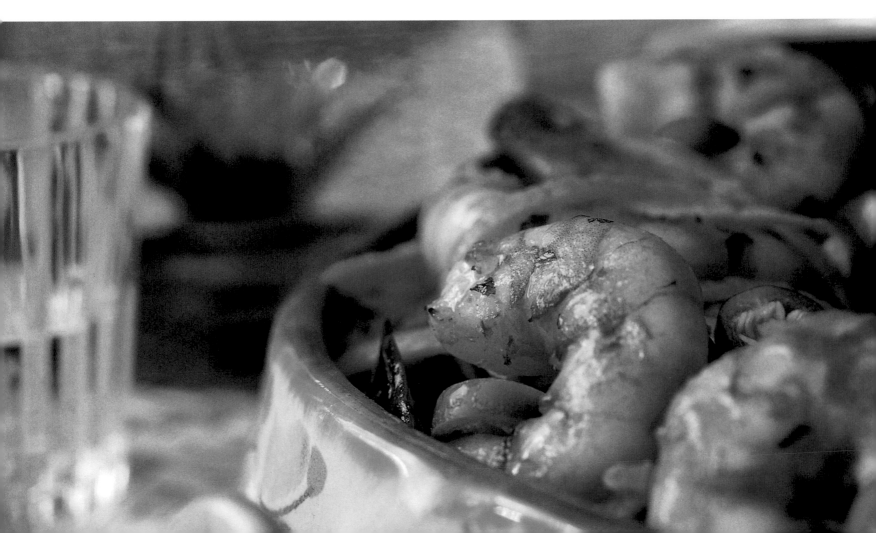

Beef medallions in drunken sauce ›

(serves 4)

For the meat:

4   filets mignon (approx. 7 ounces [200 g] each)

8   tablespoons (approx.) *pasilla* chile seeds

       oil

Spread the chile seeds on a table and roll the outer rim of each filet in the seeds, ensuring they stick well to the meat. Heat a little oil on a griddle and fry the filets for the desired time.

For the sauce:

1   ounce (25g) *pasilla* chiles

1   cup orange juice

1   clove of garlic, chopped

1/4   cup tequila

1   tablespoon olive oil

3   tablespoons chopped onion

2 1/2   ounces (75 g) *panela* cheese, crumbled

1/2   teaspoon salt (or to taste)

Clean the chiles, removing the stem and the seeds. Roast them gently on a *comal* or cast-iron griddle. Place the chiles in a blender with the garlic and orange juice. Blend for a few minutes, then pour into a salsa bowl and mix in the tequila, olive oil, onions, cheese, and salt.

Top: Beef medallions in drunken sauce

Loin of pork with prunes

(serves 4)

1 2/3 pound (3/4 kg) pork loin

10   prunes

4   tablespoons oil

1/2   cup finely sliced leeks

2   cloves

2   allspice

1   cinnamon stick (4 cm)

2   small bay leaves

1   small sprig of thyme

1/2   cup tequila

1   cup orange juice

1   cup water

1   teaspoon Bovril, salt, and pepper

Stuff the pork loin with the prunes, rub salt and pepper over the meat, and brown on all sides in hot oil in a casserole. Place on top the leeks, cloves, allspice, cinnamon stick, bay leaves, and thyme, and put in a preheated (280°F) oven for 20 minutes. Remove from the oven, pour the tequila over, and set alight. Return the casserole to the oven for 30 minutes more, basting two or three times with the stock. Then remove from the oven and strain the sauce, squeezing as much liquid as possible from the solids. Slice the pork loin, arrange on a serving dish, and pour the sauce on top.

Marbled chocolate dessert

(serves 6)

2	slabs (18 ounces [50 g] each) table chocolate
1	cup whipping cream
3	tablespoons tequila
2	tablespoons confectioners' (icing) sugar

In the top of a double boiler, melt the chocolate with 2 tablespoons of whipping cream and the tequila, stirring well. Remove from the heat and allow to cool.

Beat the rest of the cream until stiff and mix in the sugar. Carefully fold in the chocolate so a marbled effect is achieved. Serve in a glass bowl.

Mousse Margarita

(serves 8)

2	teaspoons plain gelatin
1/2	cup sugar
	pinch of salt
4	eggs, separated
4	tablespoons lime juice
2	tablespoons water
1/2	cup tequila
1/4	cup triple sec
1/2	cup sugar
	grating of lime peel
	few drops green vegetable coloring

In a medium casserole, mix together the gelatin, 1/2 cup sugar, and pinch of salt. In a large bowl, beat the egg yolks until thick and creamy. Add the lime juice and water and mix well together. Pour over the gelatin, then place over medium heat, stirring until dissolved. Remove from the heat and add the tequila, triple sec, lime gratings, and drops of green food coloring, mixing well.

In a large bowl, beat the egg whites until stiff, then add slowly the other 1/2 cup of sugar. When the tequila mixture begins to set, fold in the egg whites. Serve in a large glass bowl or individual glasses, decorated with orange blossoms.

Right: *Mousse Margarita*

Notes

1. A song composed by E. Cortázar 60 years ago about the nature of tequila. Cocula and Tecalitlán are two municipalities in Jalisco. San Pedro refers to San Pedro Tlaquepaque, a municipality that today borders Guadalajara. The famous traditions of Tlaquepaque are their craftsmanship in clay and blown glass, their mariachi music, and the best prepared goat—called *birria*—and veal in the country.

2. Mayahuel, goddess of fertility and of the maguey, had several husbands and 400 sons. All of the sons were rabbits. The second son was called Ome Tochtli (*ome*, "two," and *tochtli*, "rabbit"; that is, "Rabbit Number Two"). Two Rabbit is actually a date in the Aztec calendar. Mexicans used to assign a certain rabbit-scale to drunkenness, from a very mild one (say, a few rabbits) to the very special one, with 400 rabbits, meaning you were about to talk with the gods.

3. Now used interchangeably, these two words, *maguey* and *agave*, lead to confusion. The simplest way out is to accept that many varieties of the maguey or agave plants produce pulque and all the non-tequila mescals, while only the very special *Agave tequilana Weber azul* (blue agave) produces tequila.

4. Tequila that is bottled and exported to the United States must have a maximum of 40 degrees GL. In Europe there is no limit, though it is commonly set at 38 degrees GL since superior gradations are subject to higher taxes.

5. It is a general practice to age tequila in barrels that once contained Kentucky bourbon. Cognac barrels are also used.

6. Officially, Tequila was not always called by this name and was considered a small settlement instead of a village. In 1656, it was called Villa de Torres Argos de Ulloa y Chávez, in honor of the governor of the kingdom of "Nueva Galicia." In 1785 it was inhabited by "60 Spaniards, 80 Indians and 162 helpers."

7. Don Felipe Gómez Arámbula, an employee at the Federal Electrical Commission in Tequila, Jalisco, gave us copies of his personal notes and documents from both the Tequila library and the Municipal Ministry of Amatitán library.

8. There was probably a previous La Rojeña, thought to have been founded by Nicolás Rojas before 1750, but the relationship between the two Rojas is unclear. Perhaps they were father and son.

9. The remaining 45 percent belongs to foreign companies like Grand Metropolitan of the United Kingdom (now part of Diageo). The association between tequila manufacturers and international distributors is explained later in the book.

10. La Gallardeña belonged to Mr. Gallardo. His granddaughter and great granddaughter inherited Cuervo. A song tells us that "they all were witches," but they were in fact alchemists who inhabited Tequila, Jalisco, and its surroundings.

11. These barrels, called *botijas*, were round clay containers each of which could hold the equivalent of seven of today's barrels.

12. Grand Metropolitan, now part of Diageo, is Cuervo's main distributor.

13. A company associated with Hiram Walker and Sons and part of the gigantic English and Spanish consortium Allied Domecq. This firm manages all of Sauza's exports.

14. Tequila Cuervo, S.A. de C.V. (La Rojeña factory), authorized to use the regulation NOM 1104.

15. Casa Cuervo, S.A. de C.V., NOM 1122.

16. The Orendain family founded many distilleries in this century in Tequila as well as in other municipalities of Jalisco. Today each of the Orendain brothers has his own distillery, though the firm is handled like a consortium. One of these brothers, Carlos Orendain, is the current president of the Regional Tequila Chamber.

17. Or La Cofradía, a similar company that performs much the same kind of service.

18. This distillery became two factories belonging to Tequila 7 Leguas, discussed later in the text.

19. Fernando signs his name "7 González" because he is the seventh son.

20. Bob Emmons: *The Book of Tequila: A Complete Guide* (Chicago: Open Court, 1997), 183.

21. Also the name of the large forest in Jalisco that covers scores of hectares. Today it is a national reserve.

22. See the ratings in the final chapter. The others are 7 Leguas Blanco and Herradura Blanco.

23. Official norm NOM-006 of the Ministry of Commerce and Industrial Development, Federal Government, 1994.

24. Exceptions apply to bottled tequila that will be exported.

25. Bottles that are exported also have to conform to commercial agreements, such as NAFTA. Often, the content is also marked in ounces.

26. A cucurbit, a fruit of the squash family, can be used as a stiff receptacle when the skin is dried. It was common to store mescal and other liquids in these containers.

27. Pedro Infante said this to his servant in Ismael Rodríguez's movie *Los Tres García*.

Recently manufacturers have begun to make this bottle again, perhaps because it revives the nostalgia for the movies made during the Época de Oro, the "golden age" of Mexican movies.

28. *"In axcan aocmo in A mazteca, ye an Mexica. Oncan oquin nacazpotonique inic oqui cuique ini toca in Mexica."* The translation is taken from the original manuscript by Don J. Fernando Ramírez and quoted from Vicente Riva Palacio et al., *México a través de los siglos* (facsimile ed., Editorial Cumbre, 1984), vol. 2.

29. He sanctioned a massive execution. During his trial, Hidalgo was interrogated and asked why he had allowed these people to be killed without a trial. He answered, "Why judge them, since they were all innocent."

30. Today, the Mexican *charro* cowboys have modified their dress. They use their gala costumes only for special occasions and a simple, elegant one for other events. This is because they do not want to be mistaken for mariachis.

31. One traditional dish is *chiles en nogada*, a recipe made of *poblano* chile filled with a sweet ground beef, covered in a nougat of white cream, and decorated with pomegranate seeds, thereby replicating the colors of the Mexican flag.

32. The Ministry of Tequila is a URL on the Internet, a site visited by many tequila fans who want to post their experiences and recommendations, etc. On one of its pages is posted Francisco Morales's obituary, along with an article on his invention of the margarita cocktail. The address is:

http://www.meteorite.net/tequila

TEQUILA
The Spirit of Mexico